50 New Year's Recipes for Home

By: Kelly Johnson

Table of Contents

- Classic Chicken Pot Pie
- Beef and Mushroom Pot Pie
- Turkey and Vegetable Pot Pie
- Spinach and Feta Pot Pie
- Ham and Cheese Pot Pie
- Shrimp and Corn Pot Pie
- Salmon Pot Pie
- Lobster Pot Pie
- Vegetable Pot Pie
- Lentil and Potato Pot Pie
- Sausage and Pepper Pot Pie
- Steak and Ale Pot Pie
- Tofu and Vegetable Pot Pie
- Crab Pot Pie
- Eggplant and Tomato Pot Pie
- Pork and Apple Pot Pie
- Curry Chicken Pot Pie
- Shepherd's Pie
- Ratatouille Pot Pie
- Tex-Mex Chicken Pot Pie
- Cauliflower and Cheese Pot Pie
- Black Bean and Corn Pot Pie
- Sweet Potato and Black Bean Pot Pie
- Chicken and Dumpling Pot Pie
- Mediterranean Vegetable Pot Pie
- Buffalo Chicken Pot Pie
- Potato and Leek Pot Pie
- Turkey and Cranberry Pot Pie
- Broccoli and Cheddar Pot Pie
- Italian Sausage and Pepper Pot Pie
- Chicken and Bacon Pot Pie
- Pumpkin and Sage Pot Pie
- Beef and Guinness Pot Pie
- Mushroom and Leek Pot Pie
- Chicken and Asparagus Pot Pie

- Gumbo Pot Pie
- Quinoa and Vegetable Pot Pie
- Pesto Chicken Pot Pie
- Ratatouille Pot Pie
- Corned Beef and Cabbage Pot Pie
- Chicken and Spinach Pot Pie
- Coconut Curry Vegetable Pot Pie
- Apple and Cheddar Pot Pie
- Artichoke and Spinach Pot Pie
- Chicken and Broccoli Pot Pie
- Chorizo and Potato Pot Pie
- Teriyaki Chicken Pot Pie
- Greek Lamb Pot Pie
- Macaroni and Cheese Pot Pie
- Thai Red Curry Chicken Pot Pie

Classic Chicken Pot Pie

Ingredients:

- 2 pie crusts (store-bought or homemade)
- 2 cups cooked chicken, diced
- 1 cup frozen mixed vegetables (carrots, peas, corn)
- 1/3 cup butter
- 1/3 cup chopped onion
- 1/3 cup all-purpose flour
- 1/2 teaspoon salt
- 1/4 teaspoon black pepper
- 1/4 teaspoon dried thyme
- 1 3/4 cups chicken broth
- 2/3 cup milk

Instructions:

Preheat your oven to 425°F (220°C).

Roll out one pie crust and place it in a 9-inch pie dish. Press the crust into the bottom and up the sides of the dish. Trim any excess crust hanging over the edge.

In a large skillet, melt the butter over medium heat. Add the chopped onion and cook until softened, about 3-4 minutes.

Stir in the flour, salt, pepper, and thyme, cooking for another 1-2 minutes until the mixture is well combined and slightly golden.

Slowly whisk in the chicken broth and milk, stirring constantly to prevent lumps from forming. Cook until the mixture thickens and bubbles.

Add the cooked chicken and mixed vegetables to the skillet, stirring until everything is evenly coated with the sauce. Remove from heat.

Pour the chicken and vegetable mixture into the prepared pie crust.

Roll out the second pie crust and place it over the filling. Trim any excess crust and crimp the edges to seal the pie.

Cut a few slits in the top crust to allow steam to escape during baking.

Optional: Brush the top crust with a beaten egg for a shiny finish.

Place the pie on a baking sheet (to catch any drips) and bake in the preheated oven for 30-35 minutes, or until the crust is golden brown and the filling is bubbling.

Allow the pot pie to cool for a few minutes before slicing and serving.

Enjoy your classic chicken pot pie!

Beef and Mushroom Pot Pie

Ingredients:

- 1 pound beef stew meat, cut into small cubes
- Salt and black pepper to taste
- 2 tablespoons olive oil
- 1 onion, diced
- 2 cloves garlic, minced
- 8 ounces mushrooms, sliced
- 2 carrots, diced
- 2 celery stalks, diced
- 1/4 cup all-purpose flour
- 2 cups beef broth
- 1 teaspoon Worcestershire sauce
- 1 teaspoon dried thyme
- 1 teaspoon dried rosemary
- 1/2 cup frozen peas
- 1/2 cup frozen corn
- 1 refrigerated pie crust or homemade pie crust

Instructions:

Preheat your oven to 375°F (190°C).
Season the beef stew meat with salt and black pepper.
Heat olive oil in a large skillet over medium-high heat. Add the seasoned beef cubes and cook until browned on all sides, about 5-7 minutes. Remove the beef from the skillet and set aside.
In the same skillet, add diced onion and cook until softened, about 3-4 minutes. Add minced garlic and cook for another 1-2 minutes.
Add sliced mushrooms, diced carrots, and diced celery to the skillet. Cook until vegetables are tender, about 5-7 minutes.
Sprinkle flour over the vegetables in the skillet and stir to coat evenly. Cook for 1-2 minutes.
Slowly pour in beef broth while stirring continuously to prevent lumps from forming. Add Worcestershire sauce, dried thyme, and dried rosemary. Bring to a simmer and cook until the sauce thickens, about 5 minutes.
Stir in the browned beef cubes, frozen peas, and frozen corn. Remove from heat.

Transfer the beef and vegetable mixture into a 9-inch pie dish.
Roll out the pie crust and place it over the filling in the pie dish. Trim any excess crust and crimp the edges to seal the pie.
Cut a few slits in the top crust to allow steam to escape during baking.
Optional: Brush the top crust with a beaten egg for a shiny finish.
Place the pie on a baking sheet (to catch any drips) and bake in the preheated oven for 30-35 minutes, or until the crust is golden brown and the filling is bubbling.
Allow the pot pie to cool for a few minutes before slicing and serving.

Enjoy your hearty beef and mushroom pot pie!

Turkey and Vegetable Pot Pie

Ingredients:

- 2 cups cooked turkey, diced
- 2 tablespoons unsalted butter
- 1 onion, diced
- 2 cloves garlic, minced
- 2 carrots, diced
- 2 celery stalks, diced
- 1 cup frozen peas
- 1 cup frozen corn
- 1/4 cup all-purpose flour
- 2 cups chicken or turkey broth
- 1/2 cup heavy cream
- 1 teaspoon dried thyme
- 1 teaspoon dried rosemary
- Salt and black pepper to taste
- 1 refrigerated pie crust or homemade pie crust

Instructions:

Preheat your oven to 375°F (190°C).
In a large skillet, melt the butter over medium heat. Add diced onion and cook until softened, about 3-4 minutes. Add minced garlic and cook for another 1-2 minutes.
Add diced carrots and diced celery to the skillet. Cook until vegetables are tender, about 5-7 minutes.
Stir in frozen peas and frozen corn. Cook for an additional 2-3 minutes.
Sprinkle flour over the vegetables in the skillet and stir to coat evenly. Cook for 1-2 minutes.
Slowly pour in chicken or turkey broth while stirring continuously to prevent lumps from forming. Add heavy cream, dried thyme, dried rosemary, salt, and black pepper. Bring to a simmer and cook until the sauce thickens, about 5 minutes.
Stir in diced turkey meat until evenly distributed. Remove from heat.
Transfer the turkey and vegetable mixture into a 9-inch pie dish.
Roll out the pie crust and place it over the filling in the pie dish. Trim any excess crust and crimp the edges to seal the pie.

Cut a few slits in the top crust to allow steam to escape during baking.
Optional: Brush the top crust with a beaten egg for a shiny finish.
Place the pie on a baking sheet (to catch any drips) and bake in the preheated oven for 30-35 minutes, or until the crust is golden brown and the filling is bubbling.
Allow the pot pie to cool for a few minutes before slicing and serving.

Enjoy your comforting turkey and vegetable pot pie!

Spinach and Feta Pot Pie

Ingredients:

- 1 refrigerated pie crust or homemade pie crust
- 2 tablespoons olive oil
- 1 onion, diced
- 2 cloves garlic, minced
- 6 cups fresh spinach leaves, chopped
- 1 cup crumbled feta cheese
- 1/4 cup grated Parmesan cheese
- 1/4 cup all-purpose flour
- 1 cup milk
- Salt and black pepper to taste
- Pinch of nutmeg (optional)

Instructions:

Preheat your oven to 375°F (190°C).
In a large skillet, heat olive oil over medium heat. Add diced onion and cook until softened, about 3-4 minutes. Add minced garlic and cook for another 1-2 minutes.
Add chopped spinach to the skillet and cook until wilted, about 2-3 minutes.
Stir in crumbled feta cheese and grated Parmesan cheese until well combined.
Sprinkle flour over the spinach mixture in the skillet and stir to coat evenly. Cook for 1-2 minutes.
Slowly pour in milk while stirring continuously to prevent lumps from forming.
Add salt, black pepper, and a pinch of nutmeg if desired. Bring to a simmer and cook until the sauce thickens, about 3-4 minutes.
Remove the skillet from heat and let the filling cool slightly.
Transfer the spinach and feta mixture into a 9-inch pie dish.
Roll out the pie crust and place it over the filling in the pie dish. Trim any excess crust and crimp the edges to seal the pie.
Cut a few slits in the top crust to allow steam to escape during baking.
Optional: Brush the top crust with a beaten egg for a shiny finish.
Place the pie on a baking sheet (to catch any drips) and bake in the preheated oven for 25-30 minutes, or until the crust is golden brown and the filling is bubbly.
Allow the pot pie to cool for a few minutes before slicing and serving.

Enjoy your delicious spinach and feta pot pie!

Ham and Cheese Pot Pie

Ingredients:

- 1 refrigerated pie crust or homemade pie crust
- 2 tablespoons unsalted butter
- 1/4 cup all-purpose flour
- 1 1/2 cups milk
- 1 cup diced cooked ham
- 1 cup shredded cheddar cheese
- 1 cup frozen peas
- 1/2 cup diced bell peppers (any color)
- 1/4 cup diced onion
- Salt and black pepper to taste
- Pinch of paprika (optional)

Instructions:

Preheat your oven to 375°F (190°C).
In a large skillet, melt the butter over medium heat. Add diced onion and diced bell peppers. Cook until softened, about 3-4 minutes.
Stir in the diced ham and cook for another 2-3 minutes until heated through.
Sprinkle flour over the ham and vegetable mixture in the skillet and stir to coat evenly. Cook for 1-2 minutes.
Slowly pour in milk while stirring continuously to prevent lumps from forming. Bring to a simmer and cook until the sauce thickens, about 3-4 minutes.
Stir in shredded cheddar cheese until melted and smooth. Season with salt and black pepper to taste.
Add frozen peas to the skillet and cook for an additional 2-3 minutes until heated through.
Remove the skillet from heat and let the filling cool slightly.
Transfer the ham and cheese mixture into a 9-inch pie dish.
Roll out the pie crust and place it over the filling in the pie dish. Trim any excess crust and crimp the edges to seal the pie.
Cut a few slits in the top crust to allow steam to escape during baking.
Optional: Sprinkle a pinch of paprika over the top crust for extra flavor and color.
Place the pie on a baking sheet (to catch any drips) and bake in the preheated oven for 25-30 minutes, or until the crust is golden brown and the filling is bubbly.
Allow the pot pie to cool for a few minutes before slicing and serving.

Enjoy your savory ham and cheese pot pie!

Shrimp and Corn Pot Pie

Ingredients:

- 1 refrigerated pie crust or homemade pie crust
- 2 tablespoons unsalted butter
- 1/4 cup all-purpose flour
- 1 1/2 cups chicken or seafood broth
- 1 cup milk
- 1 pound shrimp, peeled and deveined, tails removed
- 1 cup frozen corn kernels
- 1/2 cup diced red bell pepper
- 1/2 cup diced onion
- 2 cloves garlic, minced
- 1/4 cup chopped fresh parsley
- Salt and black pepper to taste
- Pinch of cayenne pepper (optional)
- 1 tablespoon lemon juice

Instructions:

Preheat your oven to 375°F (190°C).
In a large skillet, melt the butter over medium heat. Add diced onion and diced red bell pepper. Cook until softened, about 3-4 minutes.
Add minced garlic and cook for another 1-2 minutes until fragrant.
Sprinkle flour over the vegetable mixture in the skillet and stir to coat evenly. Cook for 1-2 minutes.
Slowly pour in chicken or seafood broth and milk while stirring continuously to prevent lumps from forming. Bring to a simmer and cook until the sauce thickens, about 3-4 minutes.
Stir in frozen corn kernels and cook for 2-3 minutes.
Add shrimp to the skillet and cook until they turn pink and opaque, about 3-4 minutes.
Stir in chopped fresh parsley and lemon juice. Season with salt, black pepper, and a pinch of cayenne pepper if desired. Taste and adjust seasoning if necessary.
Remove the skillet from heat and let the filling cool slightly.
Transfer the shrimp and corn mixture into a 9-inch pie dish.

Roll out the pie crust and place it over the filling in the pie dish. Trim any excess crust and crimp the edges to seal the pie.

Cut a few slits in the top crust to allow steam to escape during baking.

Place the pie on a baking sheet (to catch any drips) and bake in the preheated oven for 25-30 minutes, or until the crust is golden brown and the filling is bubbly.

Allow the pot pie to cool for a few minutes before slicing and serving.

Enjoy your delicious shrimp and corn pot pie!

Salmon Pot Pie

Ingredients:

- 1 refrigerated pie crust or homemade pie crust
- 1 pound salmon fillet, skin removed and cut into bite-sized pieces
- Salt and black pepper to taste
- 2 tablespoons unsalted butter
- 1/4 cup all-purpose flour
- 1 1/2 cups vegetable or seafood broth
- 1 cup milk
- 1 cup frozen peas
- 1/2 cup diced carrots
- 1/2 cup diced celery
- 1/4 cup diced onion
- 2 cloves garlic, minced
- 1/4 cup chopped fresh dill (or 1 tablespoon dried dill)
- Juice of 1 lemon

Instructions:

Preheat your oven to 375°F (190°C).
Season the salmon pieces with salt and black pepper to taste.
In a large skillet, melt the butter over medium heat. Add diced onion, diced carrots, and diced celery. Cook until softened, about 3-4 minutes.
Add minced garlic and cook for another 1-2 minutes until fragrant.
Sprinkle flour over the vegetable mixture in the skillet and stir to coat evenly. Cook for 1-2 minutes.
Slowly pour in vegetable or seafood broth and milk while stirring continuously to prevent lumps from forming. Bring to a simmer and cook until the sauce thickens, about 3-4 minutes.
Stir in frozen peas and chopped fresh dill. Cook for 2-3 minutes.
Add salmon pieces to the skillet and gently fold them into the sauce. Cook until salmon is just cooked through, about 3-4 minutes. Be careful not to overcook the salmon.
Remove the skillet from heat and stir in lemon juice. Taste and adjust seasoning if necessary.
Transfer the salmon mixture into a 9-inch pie dish.

Roll out the pie crust and place it over the filling in the pie dish. Trim any excess crust and crimp the edges to seal the pie.

Cut a few slits in the top crust to allow steam to escape during baking.

Place the pie on a baking sheet (to catch any drips) and bake in the preheated oven for 25-30 minutes, or until the crust is golden brown and the filling is bubbly.

Allow the pot pie to cool for a few minutes before slicing and serving.

Enjoy your flavorful salmon pot pie!

Lobster Pot Pie

Ingredients:

- 1 refrigerated pie crust or homemade pie crust
- 2 lobster tails (about 6-8 ounces each), cooked and meat removed from shells, chopped into bite-sized pieces
- 2 tablespoons unsalted butter
- 1/4 cup all-purpose flour
- 1 1/2 cups seafood broth or clam juice
- 1 cup milk
- 1 cup frozen peas
- 1/2 cup diced carrots
- 1/2 cup diced celery
- 1/4 cup diced onion
- 2 cloves garlic, minced
- 1/4 cup chopped fresh parsley
- Salt and black pepper to taste
- Pinch of cayenne pepper (optional)
- Juice of 1 lemon

Instructions:

Preheat your oven to 375°F (190°C).
In a large skillet, melt the butter over medium heat. Add diced onion, diced carrots, and diced celery. Cook until softened, about 3-4 minutes.
Add minced garlic and cook for another 1-2 minutes until fragrant.
Sprinkle flour over the vegetable mixture in the skillet and stir to coat evenly. Cook for 1-2 minutes.
Slowly pour in seafood broth or clam juice and milk while stirring continuously to prevent lumps from forming. Bring to a simmer and cook until the sauce thickens, about 3-4 minutes.
Stir in frozen peas and chopped fresh parsley. Cook for 2-3 minutes.
Add chopped lobster meat to the skillet and gently fold it into the sauce. Cook until lobster is heated through, about 2-3 minutes. Be careful not to overcook the lobster.

Remove the skillet from heat and stir in lemon juice. Season with salt, black pepper, and a pinch of cayenne pepper if desired. Taste and adjust seasoning if necessary.

Transfer the lobster mixture into a 9-inch pie dish.

Roll out the pie crust and place it over the filling in the pie dish. Trim any excess crust and crimp the edges to seal the pie.

Cut a few slits in the top crust to allow steam to escape during baking.

Place the pie on a baking sheet (to catch any drips) and bake in the preheated oven for 25-30 minutes, or until the crust is golden brown and the filling is bubbly.

Allow the pot pie to cool for a few minutes before slicing and serving.

Enjoy your luxurious lobster pot pie!

Vegetable Pot Pie

Ingredients:

- 1 refrigerated pie crust or homemade pie crust
- 2 tablespoons unsalted butter
- 1/4 cup all-purpose flour
- 1 1/2 cups vegetable broth
- 1 cup milk (or use non-dairy milk for a vegan option)
- 2 cups mixed vegetables (such as carrots, peas, corn, green beans), fresh or frozen
- 1/2 cup diced potatoes
- 1/2 cup diced onion
- 2 cloves garlic, minced
- 1/4 cup chopped fresh parsley
- 1 teaspoon dried thyme
- Salt and black pepper to taste

Instructions:

Preheat your oven to 375°F (190°C).
In a large skillet, melt the butter over medium heat. Add diced onion and cook until softened, about 3-4 minutes. Add minced garlic and cook for another 1-2 minutes until fragrant.
Add diced potatoes and mixed vegetables to the skillet. Cook until slightly softened, about 5-7 minutes.
Sprinkle flour over the vegetable mixture in the skillet and stir to coat evenly. Cook for 1-2 minutes.
Slowly pour in vegetable broth and milk while stirring continuously to prevent lumps from forming. Bring to a simmer and cook until the sauce thickens, about 3-4 minutes.
Stir in chopped fresh parsley and dried thyme. Season with salt and black pepper to taste.
Remove the skillet from heat and let the filling cool slightly.
Transfer the vegetable mixture into a 9-inch pie dish.
Roll out the pie crust and place it over the filling in the pie dish. Trim any excess crust and crimp the edges to seal the pie.
Cut a few slits in the top crust to allow steam to escape during baking.

Place the pie on a baking sheet (to catch any drips) and bake in the preheated oven for 25-30 minutes, or until the crust is golden brown and the filling is bubbly. Allow the pot pie to cool for a few minutes before slicing and serving.

Enjoy your comforting vegetable pot pie! You can also customize the vegetables according to your preference or what you have on hand.

Lentil and Potato Pot Pie

Ingredients:

- 1 refrigerated pie crust or homemade pie crust
- 1 cup dry green or brown lentils, rinsed and drained
- 2 cups vegetable broth
- 2 tablespoons olive oil
- 1 onion, diced
- 2 cloves garlic, minced
- 2 carrots, diced
- 2 celery stalks, diced
- 2 cups diced potatoes
- 1 teaspoon dried thyme
- 1 teaspoon dried rosemary
- Salt and black pepper to taste
- 2 tablespoons all-purpose flour
- 1 cup milk (or use non-dairy milk for a vegan option)
- 1 cup frozen peas
- 1/4 cup chopped fresh parsley

Instructions:

Preheat your oven to 375°F (190°C).

In a medium saucepan, combine the lentils and vegetable broth. Bring to a boil over medium-high heat, then reduce the heat to low, cover, and simmer for 20-25 minutes, or until the lentils are tender and most of the liquid is absorbed. Drain any excess liquid and set aside.

In a large skillet, heat the olive oil over medium heat. Add diced onion and cook until softened, about 3-4 minutes. Add minced garlic and cook for another 1-2 minutes until fragrant.

Add diced carrots, diced celery, and diced potatoes to the skillet. Cook until slightly softened, about 5-7 minutes.

Stir in dried thyme, dried rosemary, salt, and black pepper to taste.

Sprinkle flour over the vegetable mixture in the skillet and stir to coat evenly. Cook for 1-2 minutes.

Slowly pour in milk while stirring continuously to prevent lumps from forming. Bring to a simmer and cook until the sauce thickens, about 3-4 minutes.

Stir in cooked lentils, frozen peas, and chopped fresh parsley. Cook for an additional 2-3 minutes.
Remove the skillet from heat and let the filling cool slightly.
Transfer the lentil and potato mixture into a 9-inch pie dish.
Roll out the pie crust and place it over the filling in the pie dish. Trim any excess crust and crimp the edges to seal the pie.
Cut a few slits in the top crust to allow steam to escape during baking.
Place the pie on a baking sheet (to catch any drips) and bake in the preheated oven for 25-30 minutes, or until the crust is golden brown and the filling is bubbly.
Allow the pot pie to cool for a few minutes before slicing and serving.

Enjoy your hearty lentil and potato pot pie!

Sausage and Pepper Pot Pie

Ingredients:

- 1 refrigerated pie crust or homemade pie crust
- 1 pound Italian sausage, casings removed
- 1 onion, thinly sliced
- 2 bell peppers (any color), thinly sliced
- 2 cloves garlic, minced
- 1 teaspoon dried oregano
- 1 teaspoon dried basil
- Salt and black pepper to taste
- 2 tablespoons all-purpose flour
- 1 cup chicken broth
- 1 cup milk
- 1 cup shredded mozzarella cheese
- 1/4 cup grated Parmesan cheese

Instructions:

Preheat your oven to 375°F (190°C).
In a large skillet, cook the Italian sausage over medium-high heat, breaking it apart with a spoon, until browned and cooked through, about 5-7 minutes. Remove the sausage from the skillet and set aside, leaving any drippings in the skillet.
In the same skillet, add sliced onion and bell peppers. Cook until softened, about 5 minutes.
Add minced garlic, dried oregano, dried basil, salt, and black pepper to the skillet. Cook for another 1-2 minutes until fragrant.
Sprinkle flour over the vegetables in the skillet and stir to coat evenly. Cook for 1-2 minutes.
Slowly pour in chicken broth and milk while stirring continuously to prevent lumps from forming. Bring to a simmer and cook until the sauce thickens, about 3-4 minutes.
Stir in cooked Italian sausage, shredded mozzarella cheese, and grated Parmesan cheese until well combined. Remove from heat.
Transfer the sausage and pepper mixture into a 9-inch pie dish.
Roll out the pie crust and place it over the filling in the pie dish. Trim any excess crust and crimp the edges to seal the pie.

Cut a few slits in the top crust to allow steam to escape during baking.
Place the pie on a baking sheet (to catch any drips) and bake in the preheated oven for 25-30 minutes, or until the crust is golden brown and the filling is bubbly. Allow the pot pie to cool for a few minutes before slicing and serving.

Enjoy your flavorful sausage and pepper pot pie!

Steak and Ale Pot Pie

Ingredients:

For the Filling:

- 1.5 lbs (680g) beef steak, such as chuck or sirloin, cut into bite-sized pieces
- 2 tablespoons all-purpose flour
- Salt and pepper to taste
- 2 tablespoons olive oil
- 1 onion, diced
- 2 cloves garlic, minced
- 2 carrots, diced
- 2 stalks celery, diced
- 1 cup (240ml) ale or stout beer
- 2 cups (480ml) beef broth
- 2 tablespoons tomato paste
- 1 teaspoon Worcestershire sauce
- 1 teaspoon dried thyme
- 1 teaspoon dried rosemary
- 1 cup (150g) frozen peas

For the Pastry Crust:

- 1 1/2 cups (180g) all-purpose flour
- 1/2 teaspoon salt
- 1/2 cup (113g) unsalted butter, cold and cubed
- 4-6 tablespoons ice water

Instructions:

Preheat your oven to 375°F (190°C).
In a large bowl, toss the beef pieces with the flour, salt, and pepper until well coated.
Heat olive oil in a large skillet or Dutch oven over medium-high heat. Add the beef pieces in batches and cook until browned on all sides. Remove the beef from the skillet and set aside.
In the same skillet, add a little more oil if needed, then add the diced onion, garlic, carrots, and celery. Cook, stirring occasionally, until the vegetables are softened, about 5-7 minutes.

Return the browned beef to the skillet. Pour in the ale or stout beer, beef broth, tomato paste, Worcestershire sauce, thyme, and rosemary. Stir to combine and bring to a simmer. Reduce the heat to low, cover, and let simmer for about 1 hour, or until the beef is tender and the sauce has thickened.

Stir in the frozen peas and cook for another 5 minutes. Adjust seasoning with salt and pepper if needed.

While the filling is simmering, prepare the pastry crust. In a large bowl, combine the flour and salt. Cut in the cold cubed butter using a pastry cutter or fork until the mixture resembles coarse crumbs. Gradually add ice water, 1 tablespoon at a time, and mix until the dough comes together.

Roll out the pastry dough on a floured surface to fit the size of your baking dish. Transfer the beef and vegetable filling into a baking dish. Cover with the rolled-out pastry dough, trimming any excess dough and crimping the edges to seal.

Cut a few slits in the pastry to allow steam to escape during baking.

Place the pot pie in the preheated oven and bake for 35-40 minutes, or until the crust is golden brown and the filling is bubbling.

Let the pot pie cool for a few minutes before serving. Enjoy your delicious steak and ale pot pie!

Feel free to adjust the recipe according to your taste preferences and dietary restrictions. You can also add other vegetables like mushrooms or potatoes for extra flavor and texture.

Tofu and Vegetable Pot Pie

Ingredients:

For the Filling:

- 1 block (14-16 oz) firm tofu, pressed and diced into small cubes
- 2 tablespoons olive oil
- 1 onion, diced
- 2 cloves garlic, minced
- 2 carrots, diced
- 2 stalks celery, diced
- 1 cup (150g) frozen peas
- 1 cup (150g) frozen corn kernels
- 1 cup (150g) frozen green beans, chopped
- 2 tablespoons all-purpose flour
- 2 cups (480ml) vegetable broth
- 1 tablespoon soy sauce or tamari
- 1 teaspoon dried thyme
- 1 teaspoon dried rosemary
- Salt and pepper to taste

For the Pastry Crust:

- 1 1/2 cups (180g) all-purpose flour
- 1/2 teaspoon salt
- 1/2 cup (113g) vegan butter or margarine, cold and cubed
- 4-6 tablespoons ice water

Instructions:

Preheat your oven to 375°F (190°C).
Heat olive oil in a large skillet or Dutch oven over medium heat. Add the diced onion and cook until softened, about 5 minutes. Add the minced garlic and cook for an additional minute.
Add the diced carrots and celery to the skillet and cook for another 5 minutes, or until slightly softened.
Add the diced tofu to the skillet and cook for 5-7 minutes, stirring occasionally, until lightly browned on all sides.
Sprinkle the flour over the tofu and vegetable mixture and stir well to coat. Cook for 1-2 minutes to remove the raw flour taste.

Gradually pour in the vegetable broth, stirring constantly to prevent lumps from forming. Add the soy sauce, dried thyme, dried rosemary, salt, and pepper. Bring the mixture to a simmer and cook for 5-7 minutes, or until the sauce has thickened slightly.

Stir in the frozen peas, corn, and green beans. Cook for another 2-3 minutes, then remove the skillet from the heat.

While the filling is cooking, prepare the pastry crust. In a large bowl, combine the flour and salt. Cut in the cold cubed vegan butter using a pastry cutter or fork until the mixture resembles coarse crumbs. Gradually add ice water, 1 tablespoon at a time, and mix until the dough comes together.

Roll out the pastry dough on a floured surface to fit the size of your baking dish. Transfer the tofu and vegetable filling into a baking dish. Cover with the rolled-out pastry dough, trimming any excess dough and crimping the edges to seal.

Cut a few slits in the pastry to allow steam to escape during baking.

Place the pot pie in the preheated oven and bake for 35-40 minutes, or until the crust is golden brown and the filling is bubbling.

Let the pot pie cool for a few minutes before serving. Enjoy your delicious tofu and vegetable pot pie!

Feel free to adjust the recipe according to your taste preferences and dietary restrictions. You can also add other vegetables or herbs for extra flavor and variety.

Crab Pot Pie

Ingredients:

For the Filling:

- 1 pound (450g) lump crabmeat, picked over for shells
- 4 tablespoons unsalted butter
- 1/2 cup diced onion
- 1/2 cup diced celery
- 1/2 cup diced bell pepper (red, green, or a combination)
- 1/4 cup all-purpose flour
- 1 1/2 cups seafood or chicken broth
- 1/2 cup heavy cream
- 1 teaspoon Old Bay seasoning (or to taste)
- Salt and pepper to taste
- 1 cup frozen peas
- 1/4 cup chopped fresh parsley

For the Pastry Crust:

- 1 1/2 cups (180g) all-purpose flour
- 1/2 teaspoon salt
- 1/2 cup (113g) unsalted butter, cold and cubed
- 4-6 tablespoons ice water

Instructions:

Preheat your oven to 375°F (190°C).

In a large skillet, melt the butter over medium heat. Add the diced onion, celery, and bell pepper. Cook, stirring occasionally, until the vegetables are softened, about 5-7 minutes.

Sprinkle the flour over the vegetables and stir well to combine. Cook for 2-3 minutes to remove the raw flour taste.

Gradually pour in the seafood or chicken broth, stirring constantly to prevent lumps from forming. Add the heavy cream and Old Bay seasoning. Bring the mixture to a simmer and cook for 5-7 minutes, or until the sauce has thickened.

Gently fold in the lump crabmeat, frozen peas, and chopped parsley. Season with salt and pepper to taste. Remove the skillet from the heat.

While the filling is cooking, prepare the pastry crust. In a large bowl, combine the flour and salt. Cut in the cold cubed butter using a pastry cutter or fork until the

mixture resembles coarse crumbs. Gradually add ice water, 1 tablespoon at a time, and mix until the dough comes together.

Roll out the pastry dough on a floured surface to fit the size of your baking dish. Transfer the crab filling into a baking dish. Cover with the rolled-out pastry dough, trimming any excess dough and crimping the edges to seal.

Cut a few slits in the pastry to allow steam to escape during baking.

Place the pot pie in the preheated oven and bake for 35-40 minutes, or until the crust is golden brown and the filling is bubbling.

Let the pot pie cool for a few minutes before serving. Enjoy your delicious crab pot pie!

Feel free to adjust the recipe according to your taste preferences. You can also add other seafood ingredients like shrimp or scallops for extra flavor.

Eggplant and Tomato Pot Pie

Ingredients:

For the Filling:

- 2 medium eggplants, diced into 1-inch cubes
- 2 tablespoons olive oil
- 1 onion, diced
- 3 cloves garlic, minced
- 2 bell peppers, diced (any color)
- 2 cups cherry tomatoes, halved
- 1 teaspoon dried oregano
- 1 teaspoon dried basil
- Salt and pepper to taste
- 1/4 cup all-purpose flour
- 1 cup vegetable broth
- 1/2 cup grated Parmesan cheese (optional)
- 1/4 cup chopped fresh basil or parsley

For the Pastry Crust:

- 1 1/2 cups (180g) all-purpose flour
- 1/2 teaspoon salt
- 1/2 cup (113g) unsalted butter, cold and cubed
- 4-6 tablespoons ice water

Instructions:

Preheat your oven to 375°F (190°C).
Place the diced eggplant in a colander and sprinkle with salt. Let sit for about 20 minutes to draw out excess moisture. Rinse the eggplant cubes under cold water and pat dry with paper towels.
In a large skillet, heat olive oil over medium heat. Add the diced onion and cook until softened, about 5 minutes. Add the minced garlic and cook for an additional minute.
Add the diced bell peppers to the skillet and cook for another 5 minutes, or until slightly softened.
Stir in the diced eggplant and cherry tomatoes. Cook, stirring occasionally, for about 10 minutes, or until the vegetables are tender.

Add the dried oregano, dried basil, salt, and pepper to the skillet. Sprinkle the flour over the vegetables and stir well to combine.

Gradually pour in the vegetable broth, stirring constantly to prevent lumps from forming. Cook for another 2-3 minutes, or until the mixture thickens slightly.

If using, stir in the grated Parmesan cheese until melted and well combined.

Remove the skillet from the heat and stir in the chopped fresh basil or parsley.

While the filling is cooking, prepare the pastry crust. In a large bowl, combine the flour and salt. Cut in the cold cubed butter using a pastry cutter or fork until the mixture resembles coarse crumbs. Gradually add ice water, 1 tablespoon at a time, and mix until the dough comes together.

Roll out the pastry dough on a floured surface to fit the size of your baking dish. Transfer the eggplant and tomato filling into a baking dish. Cover with the rolled-out pastry dough, trimming any excess dough and crimping the edges to seal.

Cut a few slits in the pastry to allow steam to escape during baking.

Place the pot pie in the preheated oven and bake for 35-40 minutes, or until the crust is golden brown and the filling is bubbling.

Let the pot pie cool for a few minutes before serving. Enjoy your delicious eggplant and tomato pot pie!

Feel free to adjust the recipe according to your taste preferences. You can also add other vegetables like zucchini or mushrooms for extra flavor and texture.

Pork and Apple Pot Pie

Ingredients:

For the Filling:

- 1 lb (450g) pork loin or shoulder, diced into bite-sized pieces
- 2 tablespoons olive oil
- 1 onion, diced
- 2 cloves garlic, minced
- 2 carrots, diced
- 2 celery stalks, diced
- 2 medium apples, peeled, cored, and diced
- 2 tablespoons all-purpose flour
- 1 cup (240ml) chicken or vegetable broth
- 1/2 cup (120ml) apple cider or apple juice
- 1 teaspoon dried thyme
- 1 teaspoon dried sage
- Salt and pepper to taste
- 1 cup frozen peas
- 1/4 cup chopped fresh parsley

For the Pastry Crust:

- 1 1/2 cups (180g) all-purpose flour
- 1/2 teaspoon salt
- 1/2 cup (113g) unsalted butter, cold and cubed
- 4-6 tablespoons ice water

Instructions:

Preheat your oven to 375°F (190°C).
In a large skillet or Dutch oven, heat the olive oil over medium heat. Add the diced pork pieces and cook until browned on all sides, about 5-7 minutes. Remove the pork from the skillet and set aside.
In the same skillet, add a little more oil if needed, then add the diced onion, garlic, carrots, and celery. Cook, stirring occasionally, until the vegetables are softened, about 5-7 minutes.
Add the diced apples to the skillet and cook for another 3-4 minutes, until slightly softened.

Sprinkle the flour over the vegetables and apples, and stir well to coat. Cook for 1-2 minutes to remove the raw flour taste.

Gradually pour in the chicken or vegetable broth and apple cider, stirring constantly to prevent lumps from forming. Add the dried thyme, dried sage, salt, and pepper. Bring the mixture to a simmer and cook for 5-7 minutes, or until the sauce has thickened.

Stir in the frozen peas and chopped fresh parsley. Return the browned pork to the skillet and stir to combine. Remove the skillet from the heat.

While the filling is cooking, prepare the pastry crust. In a large bowl, combine the flour and salt. Cut in the cold cubed butter using a pastry cutter or fork until the mixture resembles coarse crumbs. Gradually add ice water, 1 tablespoon at a time, and mix until the dough comes together.

Roll out the pastry dough on a floured surface to fit the size of your baking dish. Transfer the pork and apple filling into a baking dish. Cover with the rolled-out pastry dough, trimming any excess dough and crimping the edges to seal.

Cut a few slits in the pastry to allow steam to escape during baking.

Place the pot pie in the preheated oven and bake for 35-40 minutes, or until the crust is golden brown and the filling is bubbling.

Let the pot pie cool for a few minutes before serving. Enjoy your delicious pork and apple pot pie!

Feel free to adjust the recipe according to your taste preferences. You can also add other ingredients like potatoes or parsnips for extra flavor and texture.

Curry Chicken Pot Pie

Ingredients:

For the Filling:

- 1 lb (450g) boneless, skinless chicken breasts or thighs, diced
- 2 tablespoons vegetable oil
- 1 onion, diced
- 2 cloves garlic, minced
- 1 tablespoon curry powder (adjust to taste)
- 1 teaspoon ground turmeric
- 1 teaspoon ground cumin
- 1 teaspoon ground coriander
- 1 teaspoon paprika
- 1/2 teaspoon ground ginger
- Salt and pepper to taste
- 1 cup diced potatoes
- 1 cup diced carrots
- 1 cup frozen peas
- 2 tablespoons all-purpose flour
- 1 cup chicken broth
- 1/2 cup coconut milk
- 1 tablespoon soy sauce or fish sauce
- 1 tablespoon lemon juice
- 1/4 cup chopped fresh cilantro (optional)

For the Pastry Crust:

- 1 1/2 cups (180g) all-purpose flour
- 1/2 teaspoon salt
- 1/2 cup (113g) unsalted butter, cold and cubed
- 4-6 tablespoons ice water

Instructions:

Preheat your oven to 375°F (190°C).
In a large skillet, heat vegetable oil over medium heat. Add the diced onion and cook until softened, about 5 minutes. Add the minced garlic and cook for an additional minute.

Add the diced chicken to the skillet and cook until browned on all sides, about 5-7 minutes.

Stir in the curry powder, turmeric, cumin, coriander, paprika, ground ginger, salt, and pepper. Cook for 1-2 minutes until fragrant.

Add the diced potatoes and carrots to the skillet. Cook for another 5 minutes.

Sprinkle the flour over the chicken and vegetable mixture and stir well to coat. Cook for 1-2 minutes to remove the raw flour taste.

Gradually pour in the chicken broth, coconut milk, soy sauce or fish sauce, and lemon juice. Stir well to combine and bring to a simmer. Cook for 5-7 minutes, or until the sauce has thickened slightly.

Stir in the frozen peas and chopped cilantro, if using. Remove the skillet from the heat.

While the filling is cooking, prepare the pastry crust. In a large bowl, combine the flour and salt. Cut in the cold cubed butter using a pastry cutter or fork until the mixture resembles coarse crumbs. Gradually add ice water, 1 tablespoon at a time, and mix until the dough comes together.

Roll out the pastry dough on a floured surface to fit the size of your baking dish. Transfer the curry chicken filling into a baking dish. Cover with the rolled-out pastry dough, trimming any excess dough and crimping the edges to seal.

Cut a few slits in the pastry to allow steam to escape during baking.

Place the pot pie in the preheated oven and bake for 35-40 minutes, or until the crust is golden brown and the filling is bubbling.

Let the pot pie cool for a few minutes before serving. Enjoy your delicious curry chicken pot pie!

Feel free to adjust the recipe according to your taste preferences and dietary restrictions. You can also add other vegetables like bell peppers or green beans for extra flavor and texture.

Shepherd's Pie

Ingredients:

For the Filling:

- 1 lb (450g) ground lamb or beef (you can also use ground chicken or turkey)
- 1 onion, diced
- 2 cloves garlic, minced
- 2 carrots, diced
- 1 cup frozen peas
- 1 cup corn kernels (fresh, canned, or frozen)
- 2 tablespoons tomato paste
- 1 cup beef or vegetable broth
- 1 tablespoon Worcestershire sauce
- 1 teaspoon dried thyme
- Salt and pepper to taste
- 2 tablespoons olive oil

For the Mashed Potato Topping:

- 2 lbs (about 1 kg) potatoes, peeled and cut into chunks
- 4 tablespoons butter
- 1/4 cup milk or cream
- Salt and pepper to taste
- 1/2 cup shredded cheddar cheese (optional)

Instructions:

Preheat your oven to 375°F (190°C).

In a large skillet, heat olive oil over medium heat. Add the diced onion and cook until softened, about 5 minutes. Add the minced garlic and cook for another minute.

Add the ground meat to the skillet and cook until browned, breaking it up with a spoon as it cooks.

Stir in the diced carrots, frozen peas, and corn kernels. Cook for another 5 minutes, or until the vegetables are slightly softened.

Add the tomato paste, beef or vegetable broth, Worcestershire sauce, dried thyme, salt, and pepper. Stir well to combine. Let the mixture simmer for 10-15 minutes, or until the sauce has thickened slightly. Adjust seasoning if needed.

While the filling is simmering, prepare the mashed potato topping. Place the peeled and chopped potatoes in a large pot of salted water. Bring to a boil and cook until the potatoes are tender, about 15-20 minutes.

Drain the potatoes and return them to the pot. Add the butter and milk or cream. Mash the potatoes until smooth and creamy. Season with salt and pepper to taste.

Transfer the meat and vegetable filling into a baking dish. Spread the mashed potatoes evenly over the top of the filling.

If desired, sprinkle shredded cheddar cheese over the mashed potatoes.

Place the Shepherd's Pie in the preheated oven and bake for 25-30 minutes, or until the mashed potatoes are golden and the filling is bubbling.

Let the Shepherd's Pie cool for a few minutes before serving. Enjoy this comforting and hearty dish!

Feel free to customize the recipe by adding other vegetables, herbs, or spices to the filling according to your taste preferences.

Ratatouille Pot Pie

Ingredients:

For the Ratatouille Filling:

- 2 tablespoons olive oil
- 1 onion, diced
- 3 cloves garlic, minced
- 1 eggplant, diced
- 2 zucchini, diced
- 1 bell pepper, diced
- 2 cups cherry tomatoes, halved
- 1 teaspoon dried thyme
- 1 teaspoon dried oregano
- Salt and pepper to taste
- 1/4 cup chopped fresh basil
- 1/4 cup tomato sauce or crushed tomatoes

For the Pot Pie Crust:

- 1 1/2 cups (180g) all-purpose flour
- 1/2 teaspoon salt
- 1/2 cup (113g) unsalted butter, cold and cubed
- 4-6 tablespoons ice water

Instructions:

Preheat your oven to 375°F (190°C).
In a large skillet, heat olive oil over medium heat. Add the diced onion and cook until softened, about 5 minutes. Add the minced garlic and cook for an additional minute.
Add the diced eggplant, zucchini, bell pepper, and cherry tomatoes to the skillet. Cook, stirring occasionally, for about 10 minutes, or until the vegetables are tender.
Stir in the dried thyme, dried oregano, salt, and pepper. Add the chopped fresh basil and tomato sauce or crushed tomatoes. Cook for another 5 minutes, then remove the skillet from the heat.
While the ratatouille filling is cooking, prepare the pot pie crust. In a large bowl, combine the flour and salt. Cut in the cold cubed butter using a pastry cutter or

fork until the mixture resembles coarse crumbs. Gradually add ice water, 1 tablespoon at a time, and mix until the dough comes together.

Roll out the pastry dough on a floured surface to fit the size of your baking dish. Transfer the ratatouille filling into a baking dish. Cover with the rolled-out pastry dough, trimming any excess dough and crimping the edges to seal.

Cut a few slits in the pastry to allow steam to escape during baking.

Place the pot pie in the preheated oven and bake for 35-40 minutes, or until the crust is golden brown and the filling is bubbling.

Let the pot pie cool for a few minutes before serving. Enjoy your delicious ratatouille pot pie!

Feel free to adjust the recipe according to your taste preferences. You can also add other vegetables like mushrooms or carrots for extra flavor and texture. Additionally, you can sprinkle grated cheese on top of the ratatouille filling before adding the crust if desired.

Tex-Mex Chicken Pot Pie

Ingredients:

For the Filling:

- 2 cups cooked chicken, shredded or diced
- 1 tablespoon olive oil
- 1 onion, diced
- 2 cloves garlic, minced
- 1 bell pepper, diced
- 1 jalapeño pepper, diced (optional, for heat)
- 1 cup corn kernels (fresh, canned, or frozen)
- 1 cup black beans, drained and rinsed
- 1 cup diced tomatoes (canned or fresh)
- 1 cup enchilada sauce
- 1 teaspoon ground cumin
- 1 teaspoon chili powder
- Salt and pepper to taste
- 1/4 cup chopped fresh cilantro
- 1 cup shredded Mexican blend cheese

For the Pastry Crust:

- 1 1/2 cups (180g) all-purpose flour
- 1/2 teaspoon salt
- 1/2 cup (113g) unsalted butter, cold and cubed
- 4-6 tablespoons ice water

Instructions:

Preheat your oven to 375°F (190°C).
In a large skillet, heat olive oil over medium heat. Add the diced onion, garlic, bell pepper, and jalapeño pepper (if using). Cook until softened, about 5 minutes.
Add the corn kernels, black beans, diced tomatoes, enchilada sauce, ground cumin, chili powder, salt, and pepper to the skillet. Stir well to combine.
Add the cooked chicken to the skillet and stir until all ingredients are evenly combined. Cook for another 5 minutes, allowing the flavors to meld together.
Remove the skillet from the heat and stir in the chopped fresh cilantro.
While the filling is cooking, prepare the pastry crust. In a large bowl, combine the flour and salt. Cut in the cold cubed butter using a pastry cutter or fork until the

mixture resembles coarse crumbs. Gradually add ice water, 1 tablespoon at a time, and mix until the dough comes together.

Roll out the pastry dough on a floured surface to fit the size of your baking dish.

Transfer the Tex-Mex chicken filling into a baking dish. Cover with the rolled-out pastry dough, trimming any excess dough and crimping the edges to seal.

Cut a few slits in the pastry to allow steam to escape during baking.

Sprinkle the shredded Mexican blend cheese evenly over the top of the pastry crust.

Place the pot pie in the preheated oven and bake for 35-40 minutes, or until the crust is golden brown and the filling is bubbling.

Let the pot pie cool for a few minutes before serving. Enjoy your delicious Tex-Mex Chicken Pot Pie!

Feel free to adjust the recipe according to your taste preferences. You can also add other Tex-Mex ingredients like chopped green chilies, diced avocado, or sliced black olives for extra flavor.

Cauliflower and Cheese Pot Pie

Ingredients:

For the Filling:

- 1 large head cauliflower, cut into small florets
- 2 tablespoons olive oil
- 1 onion, diced
- 2 cloves garlic, minced
- 2 carrots, diced
- 2 stalks celery, diced
- 1/4 cup all-purpose flour
- 2 cups vegetable broth
- 1 cup milk (or non-dairy milk for a vegan option)
- 2 cups shredded cheddar cheese (or vegan cheese)
- Salt and pepper to taste
- 1/4 cup chopped fresh parsley (optional)

For the Pastry Crust:

- 1 1/2 cups (180g) all-purpose flour
- 1/2 teaspoon salt
- 1/2 cup (113g) unsalted butter or vegan butter, cold and cubed
- 4-6 tablespoons ice water

Instructions:

Preheat your oven to 375°F (190°C).

Steam or boil the cauliflower florets until tender, about 5-7 minutes. Drain and set aside.

In a large skillet, heat olive oil over medium heat. Add the diced onion and cook until softened, about 5 minutes. Add the minced garlic and cook for an additional minute.

Add the diced carrots and celery to the skillet and cook for another 5 minutes, or until slightly softened.

Sprinkle the flour over the vegetables and stir well to coat. Cook for 2-3 minutes to remove the raw flour taste.

Gradually pour in the vegetable broth and milk, stirring constantly to prevent lumps from forming. Cook for 5-7 minutes, or until the mixture thickens.

Remove the skillet from the heat and stir in the shredded cheddar cheese until melted and well combined. Season with salt and pepper to taste.

Gently fold in the cooked cauliflower florets and chopped fresh parsley, if using.

While the filling is cooking, prepare the pastry crust. In a large bowl, combine the flour and salt. Cut in the cold cubed butter using a pastry cutter or fork until the mixture resembles coarse crumbs. Gradually add ice water, 1 tablespoon at a time, and mix until the dough comes together.

Roll out the pastry dough on a floured surface to fit the size of your baking dish.

Transfer the cauliflower and cheese filling into a baking dish. Cover with the rolled-out pastry dough, trimming any excess dough and crimping the edges to seal.

Cut a few slits in the pastry to allow steam to escape during baking.

Place the pot pie in the preheated oven and bake for 35-40 minutes, or until the crust is golden brown and the filling is bubbling.

Let the pot pie cool for a few minutes before serving. Enjoy your delicious cauliflower and cheese pot pie!

Feel free to adjust the recipe according to your taste preferences and dietary restrictions. You can also add other vegetables or herbs for extra flavor and variety.

Black Bean and Corn Pot Pie

Ingredients:

For the Filling:

- 2 tablespoons olive oil
- 1 onion, diced
- 2 cloves garlic, minced
- 1 bell pepper, diced (any color)
- 1 jalapeño pepper, seeded and diced (optional)
- 2 cups cooked black beans (canned or cooked from dry)
- 1 cup corn kernels (fresh, canned, or frozen)
- 1 teaspoon ground cumin
- 1 teaspoon chili powder
- 1/2 teaspoon smoked paprika
- Salt and pepper to taste
- 1 cup tomato sauce or diced tomatoes
- 1/4 cup chopped fresh cilantro (optional)
- 1 cup shredded cheese (cheddar, Monterey Jack, or a blend)

For the Pastry Crust:

- 1 1/2 cups (180g) all-purpose flour
- 1/2 teaspoon salt
- 1/2 cup (113g) unsalted butter or vegan butter, cold and cubed
- 4-6 tablespoons ice water

Instructions:

Preheat your oven to 375°F (190°C).
In a large skillet, heat olive oil over medium heat. Add the diced onion and cook until softened, about 5 minutes. Add the minced garlic, diced bell pepper, and jalapeño pepper (if using), and cook for an additional 2-3 minutes.
Stir in the cooked black beans, corn kernels, ground cumin, chili powder, smoked paprika, salt, and pepper. Cook for another 5 minutes, stirring occasionally, to allow the flavors to meld.
Add the tomato sauce or diced tomatoes to the skillet and stir to combine. Cook for an additional 2-3 minutes. Remove the skillet from the heat and stir in the chopped fresh cilantro (if using).

While the filling is cooking, prepare the pastry crust. In a large bowl, combine the flour and salt. Cut in the cold cubed butter using a pastry cutter or fork until the mixture resembles coarse crumbs. Gradually add ice water, 1 tablespoon at a time, and mix until the dough comes together.

Roll out the pastry dough on a floured surface to fit the size of your baking dish.

Transfer the black bean and corn filling into a baking dish. Sprinkle the shredded cheese evenly over the top.

Cover the filling with the rolled-out pastry dough, trimming any excess dough and crimping the edges to seal.

Cut a few slits in the pastry to allow steam to escape during baking.

Place the pot pie in the preheated oven and bake for 35-40 minutes, or until the crust is golden brown and the filling is bubbly.

Let the pot pie cool for a few minutes before serving. Enjoy your delicious black bean and corn pot pie!

Feel free to adjust the recipe according to your taste preferences. You can also add other vegetables like diced tomatoes, bell peppers, or green chilies for extra flavor and texture.

Sweet Potato and Black Bean Pot Pie

Ingredients:

For the Filling:

- 2 medium sweet potatoes, peeled and diced
- 1 can (15 ounces) black beans, drained and rinsed
- 1 cup corn kernels (fresh, frozen, or canned)
- 1 onion, diced
- 2 cloves garlic, minced
- 1 red bell pepper, diced
- 1 teaspoon ground cumin
- 1 teaspoon chili powder
- 1/2 teaspoon smoked paprika
- Salt and pepper to taste
- 2 tablespoons olive oil
- 1 cup vegetable broth
- 1 tablespoon tomato paste
- 1 tablespoon all-purpose flour
- 1/4 cup chopped fresh cilantro (optional)

For the Pastry Crust:

- 1 1/2 cups (180g) all-purpose flour
- 1/2 teaspoon salt
- 1/2 cup (113g) unsalted butter or vegan butter, cold and cubed
- 4-6 tablespoons ice water

Instructions:

Preheat your oven to 375°F (190°C).
Place the diced sweet potatoes in a pot of boiling water and cook until fork-tender, about 8-10 minutes. Drain and set aside.
In a large skillet, heat olive oil over medium heat. Add the diced onion and cook until softened, about 5 minutes. Add the minced garlic and cook for an additional minute.
Add the diced bell pepper to the skillet and cook for another 5 minutes, or until slightly softened.
Stir in the ground cumin, chili powder, smoked paprika, salt, and pepper. Cook for another minute to toast the spices.

Sprinkle the flour over the vegetables and stir well to coat. Cook for 2-3 minutes to remove the raw flour taste.

Gradually pour in the vegetable broth, stirring constantly to prevent lumps from forming. Add the tomato paste and stir until well combined.

Add the cooked sweet potatoes, black beans, and corn kernels to the skillet. Stir to combine and cook for another 2-3 minutes. If the mixture seems too dry, you can add a little more vegetable broth.

Remove the skillet from the heat and stir in the chopped fresh cilantro, if using.

While the filling is cooking, prepare the pastry crust. In a large bowl, combine the flour and salt. Cut in the cold cubed butter using a pastry cutter or fork until the mixture resembles coarse crumbs. Gradually add ice water, 1 tablespoon at a time, and mix until the dough comes together.

Roll out the pastry dough on a floured surface to fit the size of your baking dish. Transfer the sweet potato and black bean filling into a baking dish. Cover with the rolled-out pastry dough, trimming any excess dough and crimping the edges to seal.

Cut a few slits in the pastry to allow steam to escape during baking.

Place the pot pie in the preheated oven and bake for 35-40 minutes, or until the crust is golden brown and the filling is bubbling.

Let the pot pie cool for a few minutes before serving. Enjoy your delicious sweet potato and black bean pot pie!

Feel free to adjust the recipe according to your taste preferences and dietary restrictions. You can also add other vegetables or spices for extra flavor and variety.

Chicken and Dumpling Pot Pie

Ingredients:

For the Filling:

- 2 tablespoons unsalted butter
- 1 onion, diced
- 2 carrots, diced
- 2 celery stalks, diced
- 2 cloves garlic, minced
- 1/4 cup all-purpose flour
- 2 cups chicken broth
- 1 cup milk
- 2 cups cooked chicken, shredded or diced
- 1 cup frozen peas
- Salt and pepper to taste
- 1 tablespoon chopped fresh parsley (optional)

For the Dumplings:

- 1 cup all-purpose flour
- 2 teaspoons baking powder
- 1/2 teaspoon salt
- 1/2 cup milk
- 2 tablespoons unsalted butter, melted

Instructions:

Preheat your oven to 375°F (190°C).
In a large skillet or Dutch oven, melt the butter over medium heat. Add the diced onion, carrots, and celery. Cook until the vegetables are softened, about 5-7 minutes.
Add the minced garlic to the skillet and cook for an additional minute.
Sprinkle the flour over the vegetables and stir well to coat. Cook for 1-2 minutes to remove the raw flour taste.
Gradually pour in the chicken broth and milk, stirring constantly to prevent lumps from forming. Bring the mixture to a simmer and cook for 5-7 minutes, or until thickened.
Stir in the cooked chicken and frozen peas. Season with salt and pepper to taste. If using, add the chopped fresh parsley. Remove the skillet from the heat.

In a medium bowl, whisk together the flour, baking powder, and salt for the dumplings.

Gradually add the milk and melted butter to the dry ingredients, stirring until just combined. Be careful not to overmix.

Drop spoonfuls of the dumpling batter onto the surface of the chicken mixture in the skillet, evenly spacing them out.

Transfer the skillet to the preheated oven and bake for 20-25 minutes, or until the dumplings are golden brown and cooked through.

Remove the pot pie from the oven and let it cool for a few minutes before serving.

Serve the chicken and dumpling pot pie warm, and enjoy the comforting flavors!

Feel free to customize this recipe by adding your favorite herbs or vegetables to the filling, or by using different types of protein such as turkey or tofu.

Mediterranean Vegetable Pot Pie

Ingredients:

For the Filling:

- 2 tablespoons olive oil
- 1 onion, diced
- 3 cloves garlic, minced
- 1 eggplant, diced
- 1 zucchini, diced
- 1 red bell pepper, diced
- 1 yellow bell pepper, diced
- 1 cup cherry tomatoes, halved
- 1 can (15 oz) chickpeas, drained and rinsed
- 1/2 cup sliced black olives
- 2 teaspoons dried oregano
- 1 teaspoon dried basil
- Salt and pepper to taste
- 2 tablespoons tomato paste
- 1/4 cup vegetable broth
- 1 tablespoon all-purpose flour
- 1/4 cup chopped fresh parsley

For the Pastry Crust:

- 1 1/2 cups (180g) all-purpose flour
- 1/2 teaspoon salt
- 1/2 cup (113g) unsalted butter or vegan butter, cold and cubed
- 4-6 tablespoons ice water

Instructions:

Preheat your oven to 375°F (190°C).

In a large skillet, heat olive oil over medium heat. Add the diced onion and cook until softened, about 5 minutes. Add the minced garlic and cook for an additional minute.

Add the diced eggplant, zucchini, and bell peppers to the skillet. Cook, stirring occasionally, until the vegetables are slightly softened, about 7-8 minutes.

Stir in the cherry tomatoes, chickpeas, black olives, dried oregano, dried basil, salt, and pepper. Cook for another 2-3 minutes.

In a small bowl, whisk together the tomato paste, vegetable broth, and all-purpose flour until smooth. Pour this mixture into the skillet and stir until well combined. Cook for an additional 2-3 minutes, or until the sauce has thickened slightly.

Remove the skillet from the heat and stir in the chopped fresh parsley.

While the filling is cooking, prepare the pastry crust. In a large bowl, combine the flour and salt. Cut in the cold cubed butter using a pastry cutter or fork until the mixture resembles coarse crumbs. Gradually add ice water, 1 tablespoon at a time, and mix until the dough comes together.

Roll out the pastry dough on a floured surface to fit the size of your baking dish. Transfer the Mediterranean vegetable filling into a baking dish. Cover with the rolled-out pastry dough, trimming any excess dough and crimping the edges to seal.

Cut a few slits in the pastry to allow steam to escape during baking.

Place the pot pie in the preheated oven and bake for 35-40 minutes, or until the crust is golden brown and the filling is bubbling.

Let the pot pie cool for a few minutes before serving. Enjoy your delicious Mediterranean vegetable pot pie!

Feel free to adjust the recipe according to your taste preferences and dietary restrictions. You can also add other Mediterranean ingredients like artichoke hearts, sun-dried tomatoes, or feta cheese for extra flavor.

Buffalo Chicken Pot Pie

Ingredients:

For the Filling:

- 2 cups cooked chicken, shredded or diced
- 1 cup carrots, diced
- 1 cup celery, diced
- 1 onion, diced
- 2 cloves garlic, minced
- 1/2 cup buffalo sauce (adjust to taste)
- 1/2 cup ranch or blue cheese dressing
- 1 cup frozen peas
- 1 cup chicken broth
- 2 tablespoons all-purpose flour
- Salt and pepper to taste
- 2 tablespoons olive oil

For the Pastry Crust:

- 1 1/2 cups (180g) all-purpose flour
- 1/2 teaspoon salt
- 1/2 cup (113g) unsalted butter, cold and cubed
- 4-6 tablespoons ice water

Instructions:

Preheat your oven to 375°F (190°C).
In a large skillet, heat olive oil over medium heat. Add the diced onion, carrots, and celery. Cook until softened, about 5-7 minutes.
Add the minced garlic to the skillet and cook for an additional minute.
Stir in the cooked chicken and buffalo sauce. Cook for 2-3 minutes to combine flavors.
Sprinkle the flour over the chicken and vegetable mixture. Stir well to coat evenly. Gradually pour in the chicken broth, stirring constantly to prevent lumps from forming. Cook until the mixture thickens, about 5 minutes.
Stir in the ranch or blue cheese dressing until well combined. Season with salt and pepper to taste.
Gently fold in the frozen peas. Remove the skillet from the heat.

While the filling is cooking, prepare the pastry crust. In a large bowl, combine the flour and salt. Cut in the cold cubed butter using a pastry cutter or fork until the mixture resembles coarse crumbs. Gradually add ice water, 1 tablespoon at a time, and mix until the dough comes together.

Roll out the pastry dough on a floured surface to fit the size of your baking dish. Transfer the buffalo chicken filling into a baking dish. Cover with the rolled-out pastry dough, trimming any excess dough and crimping the edges to seal.

Cut a few slits in the pastry to allow steam to escape during baking.

Place the pot pie in the preheated oven and bake for 35-40 minutes, or until the crust is golden brown and the filling is bubbling.

Let the pot pie cool for a few minutes before serving. Enjoy your delicious buffalo chicken pot pie!

Feel free to adjust the recipe according to your taste preferences. You can also add extra buffalo sauce for more heat or garnish with chopped green onions for extra flavor.

Potato and Leek Pot Piev

Ingredients:

For the Filling:

- 4 medium potatoes, peeled and diced
- 2 leeks, white and light green parts only, sliced
- 2 tablespoons butter
- 2 cloves garlic, minced
- 1/4 cup all-purpose flour
- 2 cups vegetable broth
- 1 cup milk or cream
- Salt and pepper to taste
- 1/4 teaspoon dried thyme
- 1/4 teaspoon dried rosemary
- 1 cup frozen peas (optional)
- 1/4 cup chopped fresh parsley (optional)

For the Pastry Crust:

- 1 1/2 cups (180g) all-purpose flour
- 1/2 teaspoon salt
- 1/2 cup (113g) unsalted butter, cold and cubed
- 4-6 tablespoons ice water

Instructions:

Preheat your oven to 375°F (190°C).
In a large pot, cover the diced potatoes with water and bring to a boil. Cook until the potatoes are fork-tender, about 10-12 minutes. Drain and set aside.
In a separate large skillet, melt the butter over medium heat. Add the sliced leeks and cook until softened, about 5-7 minutes.
Add the minced garlic to the skillet and cook for an additional minute.
Sprinkle the flour over the leeks and garlic, stirring well to coat evenly. Cook for 1-2 minutes to remove the raw flour taste.
Gradually pour in the vegetable broth and milk, stirring constantly to prevent lumps from forming. Cook until the mixture thickens, about 5-7 minutes.
Stir in the dried thyme, dried rosemary, salt, and pepper. Adjust seasoning to taste.

Gently fold in the cooked diced potatoes and frozen peas (if using). Remove the skillet from the heat and stir in the chopped fresh parsley, if desired.

While the filling is cooking, prepare the pastry crust. In a large bowl, combine the flour and salt. Cut in the cold cubed butter using a pastry cutter or fork until the mixture resembles coarse crumbs. Gradually add ice water, 1 tablespoon at a time, and mix until the dough comes together.

Roll out the pastry dough on a floured surface to fit the size of your baking dish. Transfer the potato and leek filling into a baking dish. Cover with the rolled-out pastry dough, trimming any excess dough and crimping the edges to seal.

Cut a few slits in the pastry to allow steam to escape during baking.

Place the pot pie in the preheated oven and bake for 35-40 minutes, or until the crust is golden brown and the filling is bubbling.

Let the pot pie cool for a few minutes before serving. Enjoy your delicious potato and leek pot pie!

Feel free to adjust the recipe according to your taste preferences. You can also add other vegetables like carrots or mushrooms for extra flavor and texture.

Turkey and Cranberry Pot Pie

Ingredients:

For the Filling:

- 2 cups cooked turkey, diced
- 1 cup cranberry sauce
- 1 onion, diced
- 2 cloves garlic, minced
- 2 carrots, diced
- 2 celery stalks, diced
- 2 tablespoons butter or olive oil
- 1/4 cup all-purpose flour
- 2 cups turkey or chicken broth
- 1/2 cup milk or cream
- Salt and pepper to taste
- 1 tablespoon chopped fresh thyme or 1 teaspoon dried thyme
- 1 tablespoon chopped fresh parsley (optional)

For the Pastry Crust:

- 1 1/2 cups (180g) all-purpose flour
- 1/2 teaspoon salt
- 1/2 cup (113g) unsalted butter, cold and cubed
- 4-6 tablespoons ice water

Instructions:

Preheat your oven to 375°F (190°C).
In a large skillet, melt the butter or heat the olive oil over medium heat. Add the diced onion, carrots, and celery. Cook until softened, about 5-7 minutes.
Add the minced garlic to the skillet and cook for an additional minute.
Stir in the cooked diced turkey and cranberry sauce. Cook for 2-3 minutes to combine flavors.
Sprinkle the flour over the turkey and vegetable mixture. Stir well to coat evenly. Gradually pour in the turkey or chicken broth and milk or cream, stirring constantly to prevent lumps from forming. Cook until the mixture thickens, about 5-7 minutes.
Season with salt, pepper, and chopped thyme. Stir in chopped parsley, if using. Remove from heat.

While the filling is cooking, prepare the pastry crust. In a large bowl, combine the flour and salt. Cut in the cold cubed butter using a pastry cutter or fork until the mixture resembles coarse crumbs. Gradually add ice water, 1 tablespoon at a time, and mix until the dough comes together.

Roll out the pastry dough on a floured surface to fit the size of your baking dish. Transfer the turkey and cranberry filling into a baking dish. Cover with the rolled-out pastry dough, trimming any excess dough and crimping the edges to seal.

Cut a few slits in the pastry to allow steam to escape during baking.

Place the pot pie in the preheated oven and bake for 35-40 minutes, or until the crust is golden brown and the filling is bubbling.

Let the pot pie cool for a few minutes before serving. Enjoy your delicious turkey and cranberry pot pie!

Feel free to adjust the recipe according to your taste preferences. You can also add other Thanksgiving leftovers like mashed potatoes or green beans for extra flavor and variety.

Broccoli and Cheddar Pot Pie

Ingredients:

For the Filling:

- 2 cups broccoli florets, chopped
- 1 onion, finely chopped
- 2 cloves garlic, minced
- 2 tablespoons butter
- 2 tablespoons all-purpose flour
- 1 1/2 cups milk
- 1 cup shredded sharp cheddar cheese
- Salt and pepper to taste
- Pinch of nutmeg (optional)

For the Pastry Crust:

- 1 1/2 cups (180g) all-purpose flour
- 1/2 teaspoon salt
- 1/2 cup (113g) unsalted butter, cold and cubed
- 4-6 tablespoons ice water

Instructions:

Preheat your oven to 375°F (190°C).

In a large skillet, melt the butter over medium heat. Add the chopped onion and cook until softened, about 5 minutes. Add the minced garlic and cook for an additional minute.

Add the chopped broccoli florets to the skillet and cook for 3-4 minutes, until slightly tender. Remove from heat and set aside.

In the same skillet, melt the remaining butter over medium heat. Stir in the flour and cook for 1-2 minutes to form a roux.

Gradually whisk in the milk, stirring constantly to prevent lumps. Cook until the mixture thickens and begins to bubble.

Remove the skillet from heat and stir in the shredded cheddar cheese until melted and smooth. Season with salt, pepper, and nutmeg if desired.

Add the cooked broccoli and onion mixture to the cheese sauce, stirring until well combined.

While the filling is cooling slightly, prepare the pastry crust. In a large bowl, combine the flour and salt. Cut in the cold cubed butter using a pastry cutter or fork until the mixture resembles coarse crumbs. Gradually add ice water, 1 tablespoon at a time, and mix until the dough comes together.

Roll out the pastry dough on a floured surface to fit the size of your baking dish. Transfer the broccoli and cheddar filling into a baking dish. Cover with the rolled-out pastry dough, trimming any excess dough and crimping the edges to seal.

Cut a few slits in the pastry to allow steam to escape during baking.

Place the pot pie in the preheated oven and bake for 35-40 minutes, or until the crust is golden brown and the filling is bubbling.

Let the pot pie cool for a few minutes before serving. Enjoy your delicious broccoli and cheddar pot pie!

Feel free to adjust the recipe according to your taste preferences. You can also add other vegetables or herbs for extra flavor and variety.

Italian Sausage and Pepper Pot Pie

Ingredients:

For the Filling:

- 1 pound (450g) Italian sausage (mild or spicy), casings removed
- 1 onion, diced
- 2 cloves garlic, minced
- 2 bell peppers (red, green, or a combination), thinly sliced
- 1 can (14.5 ounces) diced tomatoes, drained
- 1 teaspoon Italian seasoning
- Salt and pepper to taste
- 1 cup shredded mozzarella cheese
- 2 tablespoons chopped fresh basil (optional)

For the Pastry Crust:

- 1 1/2 cups (180g) all-purpose flour
- 1/2 teaspoon salt
- 1/2 cup (113g) unsalted butter, cold and cubed
- 4-6 tablespoons ice water

Instructions:

Preheat your oven to 375°F (190°C).

In a large skillet, cook the Italian sausage over medium heat, breaking it up with a spoon, until browned and cooked through, about 8-10 minutes. Remove the sausage from the skillet and set aside, leaving any drippings in the skillet.

In the same skillet with the sausage drippings, add the diced onion and cook until softened, about 5 minutes. Add the minced garlic and cook for an additional minute.

Add the sliced bell peppers to the skillet and cook for another 5 minutes, or until softened.

Stir in the drained diced tomatoes and Italian seasoning. Cook for 2-3 minutes, then return the cooked Italian sausage to the skillet. Season with salt and pepper to taste. Stir well to combine.

Remove the skillet from the heat and stir in the shredded mozzarella cheese until melted and well combined. If desired, stir in the chopped fresh basil for extra flavor.

While the filling is cooling slightly, prepare the pastry crust. In a large bowl, combine the flour and salt. Cut in the cold cubed butter using a pastry cutter or fork until the mixture resembles coarse crumbs. Gradually add ice water, 1 tablespoon at a time, and mix until the dough comes together.

Roll out the pastry dough on a floured surface to fit the size of your baking dish. Transfer the Italian sausage and pepper filling into a baking dish. Cover with the rolled-out pastry dough, trimming any excess dough and crimping the edges to seal.

Cut a few slits in the pastry to allow steam to escape during baking.

Place the pot pie in the preheated oven and bake for 35-40 minutes, or until the crust is golden brown and the filling is bubbling.

Let the pot pie cool for a few minutes before serving. Enjoy your delicious Italian sausage and pepper pot pie!

Feel free to adjust the recipe according to your taste preferences. You can also add other ingredients like mushrooms or olives for extra flavor.

Chicken and Bacon Pot Pie

Ingredients:

For the Filling:

- 2 cups cooked chicken, shredded or diced
- 6 slices bacon, cooked and chopped
- 1 onion, diced
- 2 cloves garlic, minced
- 2 carrots, diced
- 2 stalks celery, diced
- 1 cup frozen peas
- 2 tablespoons butter
- 2 tablespoons all-purpose flour
- 1 1/2 cups chicken broth
- 1/2 cup heavy cream
- Salt and pepper to taste
- 1 tablespoon chopped fresh thyme (or 1 teaspoon dried thyme)
- 1 tablespoon chopped fresh parsley

For the Pastry Crust:

- 1 1/2 cups (180g) all-purpose flour
- 1/2 teaspoon salt
- 1/2 cup (113g) unsalted butter, cold and cubed
- 4-6 tablespoons ice water

Instructions:

Preheat your oven to 375°F (190°C).
In a large skillet, melt the butter over medium heat. Add the diced onion, carrots, and celery. Cook until softened, about 5 minutes.
Add the minced garlic to the skillet and cook for an additional minute.
Stir in the cooked chicken and chopped bacon. Cook for 2-3 minutes to combine flavors.
Sprinkle the flour over the chicken and vegetable mixture. Stir well to coat evenly.
Gradually pour in the chicken broth and heavy cream, stirring constantly to prevent lumps from forming. Cook until the mixture thickens, about 5 minutes.

Stir in the frozen peas, chopped fresh thyme, and chopped fresh parsley. Season with salt and pepper to taste.

While the filling is cooking, prepare the pastry crust. In a large bowl, combine the flour and salt. Cut in the cold cubed butter using a pastry cutter or fork until the mixture resembles coarse crumbs. Gradually add ice water, 1 tablespoon at a time, and mix until the dough comes together.

Roll out the pastry dough on a floured surface to fit the size of your baking dish. Transfer the chicken and bacon filling into a baking dish. Cover with the rolled-out pastry dough, trimming any excess dough and crimping the edges to seal.

Cut a few slits in the pastry to allow steam to escape during baking.

Place the pot pie in the preheated oven and bake for 35-40 minutes, or until the crust is golden brown and the filling is bubbling.

Let the pot pie cool for a few minutes before serving. Enjoy your delicious chicken and bacon pot pie!

Feel free to adjust the recipe according to your taste preferences. You can also add other vegetables or herbs for extra flavor and variety.

Pumpkin and Sage Pot Pie

Ingredients:

For the Filling:

- 2 cups pumpkin puree (canned or homemade)
- 1 onion, diced
- 2 cloves garlic, minced
- 2 carrots, diced
- 2 stalks celery, diced
- 1 cup vegetable broth
- 1/2 cup heavy cream
- 2 tablespoons butter
- 2 tablespoons all-purpose flour
- 1 tablespoon chopped fresh sage (or 1 teaspoon dried sage)
- Salt and pepper to taste
- Pinch of nutmeg (optional)

For the Pastry Crust:

- 1 1/2 cups (180g) all-purpose flour
- 1/2 teaspoon salt
- 1/2 cup (113g) unsalted butter, cold and cubed
- 4-6 tablespoons ice water

Instructions:

Preheat your oven to 375°F (190°C).

In a large skillet, melt the butter over medium heat. Add the diced onion, carrots, and celery. Cook until softened, about 5 minutes.

Add the minced garlic to the skillet and cook for an additional minute.

Stir in the pumpkin puree and chopped fresh sage. Cook for 2-3 minutes to allow flavors to meld.

Sprinkle the flour over the pumpkin and vegetable mixture. Stir well to coat evenly.

Gradually pour in the vegetable broth and heavy cream, stirring constantly to prevent lumps from forming. Cook until the mixture thickens, about 5 minutes. Season with salt, pepper, and a pinch of nutmeg if desired.

While the filling is cooking, prepare the pastry crust. In a large bowl, combine the flour and salt. Cut in the cold cubed butter using a pastry cutter or fork until the

mixture resembles coarse crumbs. Gradually add ice water, 1 tablespoon at a time, and mix until the dough comes together.

Roll out the pastry dough on a floured surface to fit the size of your baking dish.

Transfer the pumpkin and sage filling into a baking dish. Cover with the rolled-out pastry dough, trimming any excess dough and crimping the edges to seal.

Cut a few slits in the pastry to allow steam to escape during baking.

Place the pot pie in the preheated oven and bake for 35-40 minutes, or until the crust is golden brown and the filling is bubbling.

Let the pot pie cool for a few minutes before serving. Enjoy your delicious pumpkin and sage pot pie!

Feel free to adjust the recipe according to your taste preferences. You can also add other vegetables or herbs for extra flavor and variety.

Beef and Guinness Pot Pie

Ingredients:

For the Filling:

- 1.5 lbs (680g) beef chuck, cut into bite-sized pieces
- Salt and pepper to taste
- 2 tablespoons all-purpose flour
- 2 tablespoons olive oil
- 1 onion, diced
- 2 cloves garlic, minced
- 2 carrots, diced
- 2 stalks celery, diced
- 1 cup (240ml) Guinness stout beer
- 2 cups (480ml) beef broth
- 2 tablespoons tomato paste
- 1 tablespoon Worcestershire sauce
- 1 teaspoon dried thyme
- 1 teaspoon dried rosemary
- 1 bay leaf
- 1 cup frozen peas

For the Pastry Crust:

- 1 1/2 cups (180g) all-purpose flour
- 1/2 teaspoon salt
- 1/2 cup (113g) unsalted butter, cold and cubed
- 4-6 tablespoons ice water

Instructions:

Preheat your oven to 375°F (190°C).
Season the beef pieces with salt and pepper, then toss with the flour until evenly coated.
Heat olive oil in a large skillet or Dutch oven over medium-high heat. Add the beef pieces in batches and cook until browned on all sides. Remove the beef from the skillet and set aside.
In the same skillet, add a little more oil if needed, then add the diced onion, garlic, carrots, and celery. Cook, stirring occasionally, until the vegetables are softened, about 5-7 minutes.

Return the browned beef to the skillet. Pour in the Guinness beer, beef broth, tomato paste, Worcestershire sauce, thyme, rosemary, and bay leaf. Stir to combine and bring to a simmer.

Reduce the heat to low, cover, and let simmer for about 1 hour, or until the beef is tender and the sauce has thickened. If the sauce is too thin, you can simmer uncovered for the last 10-15 minutes to thicken it further.

Stir in the frozen peas and cook for another 5 minutes. Adjust seasoning with salt and pepper if needed. Remove the bay leaf and discard.

While the filling is simmering, prepare the pastry crust. In a large bowl, combine the flour and salt. Cut in the cold cubed butter using a pastry cutter or fork until the mixture resembles coarse crumbs. Gradually add ice water, 1 tablespoon at a time, and mix until the dough comes together.

Roll out the pastry dough on a floured surface to fit the size of your baking dish. Transfer the beef and vegetable filling into a baking dish. Cover with the rolled-out pastry dough, trimming any excess dough and crimping the edges to seal.

Cut a few slits in the pastry to allow steam to escape during baking.

Place the pot pie in the preheated oven and bake for 35-40 minutes, or until the crust is golden brown and the filling is bubbling.

Let the pot pie cool for a few minutes before serving. Enjoy your delicious beef and Guinness pot pie!

Feel free to adjust the recipe according to your taste preferences. You can also add other vegetables like mushrooms or potatoes for extra flavor and texture.

Mushroom and Leek Pot Pie

Ingredients:

For the Filling:

- 2 tablespoons olive oil
- 3 leeks, white and light green parts only, sliced
- 1 lb (450g) mushrooms, sliced (such as button or cremini)
- 3 cloves garlic, minced
- 1/4 cup (30g) all-purpose flour
- 1 1/2 cups (360ml) vegetable broth
- 1 cup (240ml) whole milk or heavy cream
- 1 teaspoon dried thyme
- Salt and pepper to taste
- 1 cup frozen peas
- 1/4 cup chopped fresh parsley

For the Pastry Crust:

- 1 1/2 cups (180g) all-purpose flour
- 1/2 teaspoon salt
- 1/2 cup (113g) unsalted butter, cold and cubed
- 4-6 tablespoons ice water

Instructions:

Preheat your oven to 375°F (190°C).
In a large skillet, heat olive oil over medium heat. Add the sliced leeks and cook until softened, about 5 minutes.
Add the sliced mushrooms to the skillet and cook until they release their juices and become tender, about 7-8 minutes.
Stir in the minced garlic and cook for an additional minute.
Sprinkle the flour over the mushroom and leek mixture and stir well to coat evenly. Cook for 2-3 minutes to remove the raw flour taste.
Gradually pour in the vegetable broth and whole milk or heavy cream, stirring constantly to prevent lumps from forming.
Add the dried thyme, salt, and pepper to taste. Bring the mixture to a simmer and cook until thickened, about 5 minutes.
Stir in the frozen peas and chopped fresh parsley. Remove the skillet from the heat.

While the filling is cooling slightly, prepare the pastry crust. In a large bowl, combine the flour and salt. Cut in the cold cubed butter using a pastry cutter or fork until the mixture resembles coarse crumbs. Gradually add ice water, 1 tablespoon at a time, and mix until the dough comes together.

Roll out the pastry dough on a floured surface to fit the size of your baking dish. Transfer the mushroom and leek filling into a baking dish. Cover with the rolled-out pastry dough, trimming any excess dough and crimping the edges to seal.

Cut a few slits in the pastry to allow steam to escape during baking.

Place the pot pie in the preheated oven and bake for 35-40 minutes, or until the crust is golden brown and the filling is bubbling.

Let the pot pie cool for a few minutes before serving. Enjoy your delicious mushroom and leek pot pie!

Feel free to adjust the recipe according to your taste preferences. You can also add other vegetables or herbs for extra flavor and variety.

Chicken and Asparagus Pot Pie

Ingredients:

For the Filling:

- 2 cups cooked chicken, shredded or diced
- 1 bunch asparagus, trimmed and cut into bite-sized pieces
- 1 onion, diced
- 2 cloves garlic, minced
- 2 carrots, diced
- 2 stalks celery, diced
- 1 cup frozen peas
- 2 tablespoons butter
- 2 tablespoons all-purpose flour
- 1 1/2 cups chicken broth
- 1/2 cup heavy cream
- Salt and pepper to taste
- 1 tablespoon chopped fresh thyme (or 1 teaspoon dried thyme)
- 1 tablespoon chopped fresh parsley

For the Pastry Crust:

- 1 1/2 cups (180g) all-purpose flour
- 1/2 teaspoon salt
- 1/2 cup (113g) unsalted butter, cold and cubed
- 4-6 tablespoons ice water

Instructions:

Preheat your oven to 375°F (190°C).
In a large skillet, melt the butter over medium heat. Add the diced onion, carrots, and celery. Cook until softened, about 5 minutes.
Add the minced garlic to the skillet and cook for an additional minute.
Add the asparagus pieces to the skillet and cook for 2-3 minutes, until slightly tender. Remove from heat and set aside.
In the same skillet, add the cooked chicken and frozen peas. Stir to combine.
Sprinkle the flour over the chicken and vegetable mixture. Stir well to coat evenly.
Gradually pour in the chicken broth and heavy cream, stirring constantly to prevent lumps from forming. Cook until the mixture thickens, about 5 minutes.

Stir in the chopped fresh thyme and parsley. Season with salt and pepper to taste.

While the filling is cooking, prepare the pastry crust. In a large bowl, combine the flour and salt. Cut in the cold cubed butter using a pastry cutter or fork until the mixture resembles coarse crumbs. Gradually add ice water, 1 tablespoon at a time, and mix until the dough comes together.

Roll out the pastry dough on a floured surface to fit the size of your baking dish. Transfer the chicken and asparagus filling into a baking dish. Cover with the rolled-out pastry dough, trimming any excess dough and crimping the edges to seal.

Cut a few slits in the pastry to allow steam to escape during baking.

Place the pot pie in the preheated oven and bake for 35-40 minutes, or until the crust is golden brown and the filling is bubbling.

Let the pot pie cool for a few minutes before serving. Enjoy your delicious chicken and asparagus pot pie!

Feel free to adjust the recipe according to your taste preferences. You can also add other vegetables or herbs for extra flavor and variety.

Gumbo Pot Pie

Ingredients:

For the Filling:

- 1 lb (450g) Andouille sausage, sliced
- 1 lb (450g) boneless, skinless chicken thighs, diced
- 1 onion, diced
- 1 green bell pepper, diced
- 2 celery stalks, diced
- 3 cloves garlic, minced
- 1 can (14.5 oz) diced tomatoes
- 4 cups chicken broth
- 1/2 cup all-purpose flour
- 1/2 cup vegetable oil
- 1/2 cup okra, sliced (fresh or frozen)
- 1 cup frozen sliced okra (optional)
- 1 tablespoon Cajun seasoning
- 1 teaspoon dried thyme
- Salt and pepper to taste
- Cooked white rice, for serving

For the Pastry Crust:

- 1 1/2 cups (180g) all-purpose flour
- 1/2 teaspoon salt
- 1/2 cup (113g) unsalted butter, cold and cubed
- 4-6 tablespoons ice water

Instructions:

Preheat your oven to 375°F (190°C).
In a large skillet or Dutch oven, heat vegetable oil over medium heat. Add the sliced Andouille sausage and cook until browned, about 5-7 minutes. Remove the sausage from the skillet and set aside.
In the same skillet, add the diced chicken thighs and cook until browned on all sides, about 5-7 minutes. Remove the chicken from the skillet and set aside.
Add the diced onion, bell pepper, and celery to the skillet. Cook until softened, about 5 minutes. Add the minced garlic and cook for an additional minute.

Sprinkle the flour over the vegetables and stir well to coat evenly. Cook for 2-3 minutes to form a roux.

Gradually pour in the chicken broth, stirring constantly to prevent lumps. Bring the mixture to a simmer and cook until thickened, about 5 minutes.

Stir in the diced tomatoes (with their juices), sliced okra, Cajun seasoning, dried thyme, salt, and pepper. Return the cooked sausage and chicken to the skillet. Simmer for another 10-15 minutes to allow the flavors to meld together. Adjust seasoning to taste.

While the filling is simmering, prepare the pastry crust. In a large bowl, combine the flour and salt. Cut in the cold cubed butter using a pastry cutter or fork until the mixture resembles coarse crumbs. Gradually add ice water, 1 tablespoon at a time, and mix until the dough comes together.

Roll out the pastry dough on a floured surface to fit the size of your baking dish. Transfer the gumbo filling into a baking dish. Cover with the rolled-out pastry dough, trimming any excess dough and crimping the edges to seal.

Cut a few slits in the pastry to allow steam to escape during baking.

Place the pot pie in the preheated oven and bake for 35-40 minutes, or until the crust is golden brown and the filling is bubbling.

Let the pot pie cool for a few minutes before serving. Serve over cooked white rice and enjoy your delicious Gumbo Pot Pie!

Feel free to adjust the recipe according to your taste preferences. You can also add other ingredients like shrimp or crab for a seafood twist on the classic gumbo.

Quinoa and Vegetable Pot Pie

Ingredients:

For the Filling:

- 1 cup quinoa, rinsed
- 2 cups vegetable broth
- 2 tablespoons olive oil
- 1 onion, diced
- 2 cloves garlic, minced
- 2 carrots, diced
- 2 celery stalks, diced
- 1 bell pepper, diced
- 1 zucchini, diced
- 1 cup corn kernels (fresh, frozen, or canned)
- 1 cup peas (fresh or frozen)
- 1 teaspoon dried thyme
- 1 teaspoon dried rosemary
- Salt and pepper to taste
- 2 tablespoons all-purpose flour
- 1 cup milk (or non-dairy milk for a vegan option)
- 1/2 cup shredded cheese (optional)
- Chopped fresh parsley for garnish (optional)

For the Pastry Crust:

- 1 1/2 cups (180g) all-purpose flour
- 1/2 teaspoon salt
- 1/2 cup (113g) unsalted butter or vegan butter, cold and cubed
- 4-6 tablespoons ice water

Instructions:

Preheat your oven to 375°F (190°C).
In a medium saucepan, combine the quinoa and vegetable broth. Bring to a boil, then reduce the heat to low, cover, and simmer for about 15 minutes, or until the quinoa is cooked and the liquid is absorbed. Remove from heat and set aside.

In a large skillet, heat the olive oil over medium heat. Add the diced onion and cook until softened, about 5 minutes. Add the minced garlic and cook for an additional minute.

Add the diced carrots, celery, bell pepper, and zucchini to the skillet. Cook, stirring occasionally, for about 5-7 minutes, or until the vegetables are tender.

Stir in the cooked quinoa, corn kernels, peas, dried thyme, dried rosemary, salt, and pepper. Cook for another 2-3 minutes to combine flavors.

Sprinkle the flour over the vegetable mixture and stir well to coat evenly.

Gradually pour in the milk, stirring constantly to prevent lumps from forming. Cook for 2-3 minutes, or until the mixture thickens slightly. If using cheese, stir it in until melted and well combined.

While the filling is cooking, prepare the pastry crust. In a large bowl, combine the flour and salt. Cut in the cold cubed butter using a pastry cutter or fork until the mixture resembles coarse crumbs. Gradually add ice water, 1 tablespoon at a time, and mix until the dough comes together.

Roll out the pastry dough on a floured surface to fit the size of your baking dish. Transfer the quinoa and vegetable filling into a baking dish. Cover with the rolled-out pastry dough, trimming any excess dough and crimping the edges to seal.

Cut a few slits in the pastry to allow steam to escape during baking.

Place the pot pie in the preheated oven and bake for 35-40 minutes, or until the crust is golden brown and the filling is bubbling.

Let the pot pie cool for a few minutes before serving. Garnish with chopped fresh parsley if desired. Enjoy your delicious quinoa and vegetable pot pie!

Feel free to adjust the recipe according to your taste preferences and dietary restrictions. You can also add other vegetables or herbs for extra flavor and variety.

Pesto Chicken Pot Pie

Ingredients:

For the Filling:

- 2 cups cooked chicken, shredded or diced
- 1 onion, diced
- 2 cloves garlic, minced
- 2 carrots, diced
- 2 stalks celery, diced
- 1 cup frozen peas
- 2 tablespoons butter
- 2 tablespoons all-purpose flour
- 1 1/2 cups chicken broth
- 1/2 cup milk (or non-dairy milk for a creamy vegan option)
- 1/4 cup basil pesto
- Salt and pepper to taste

For the Pastry Crust:

- 1 1/2 cups (180g) all-purpose flour
- 1/2 teaspoon salt
- 1/2 cup (113g) unsalted butter or vegan butter, cold and cubed
- 4-6 tablespoons ice water

Instructions:

Preheat your oven to 375°F (190°C).
In a large skillet, melt the butter over medium heat. Add the diced onion, carrots, and celery. Cook until softened, about 5 minutes.
Add the minced garlic to the skillet and cook for an additional minute.
Sprinkle the flour over the vegetables and stir well to coat evenly. Cook for 2-3 minutes to form a roux.
Gradually pour in the chicken broth and milk, stirring constantly to prevent lumps from forming. Cook until the mixture thickens, about 5 minutes.
Stir in the basil pesto until well combined. Season with salt and pepper to taste.
Add the cooked chicken and frozen peas to the skillet. Stir to combine and cook for another 2-3 minutes, until heated through.

While the filling is cooking, prepare the pastry crust. In a large bowl, combine the flour and salt. Cut in the cold cubed butter using a pastry cutter or fork until the mixture resembles coarse crumbs. Gradually add ice water, 1 tablespoon at a time, and mix until the dough comes together.

Roll out the pastry dough on a floured surface to fit the size of your baking dish. Transfer the pesto chicken filling into a baking dish. Cover with the rolled-out pastry dough, trimming any excess dough and crimping the edges to seal.

Cut a few slits in the pastry to allow steam to escape during baking.

Place the pot pie in the preheated oven and bake for 35-40 minutes, or until the crust is golden brown and the filling is bubbling.

Let the pot pie cool for a few minutes before serving. Enjoy your delicious pesto chicken pot pie!

Feel free to adjust the recipe according to your taste preferences and dietary restrictions. You can also add other vegetables or herbs for extra flavor and variety.

Ratatouille Pot Pie

Ingredients:

For the Ratatouille Filling:

- 1 eggplant, diced
- 2 zucchini, diced
- 1 yellow bell pepper, diced
- 1 red bell pepper, diced
- 1 onion, diced
- 2 cloves garlic, minced
- 2 cups diced tomatoes (fresh or canned)
- 2 tablespoons tomato paste
- 1 teaspoon dried thyme
- 1 teaspoon dried oregano
- Salt and pepper to taste
- 2 tablespoons olive oil

For the Pastry Crust:

- 1 1/2 cups (180g) all-purpose flour
- 1/2 teaspoon salt
- 1/2 cup (113g) unsalted butter or vegan butter, cold and cubed
- 4-6 tablespoons ice water

Instructions:

Preheat your oven to 375°F (190°C).

In a large skillet, heat the olive oil over medium heat. Add the diced onion and cook until softened, about 5 minutes. Add the minced garlic and cook for an additional minute.

Add the diced eggplant, zucchini, and bell peppers to the skillet. Cook, stirring occasionally, for about 10 minutes, or until the vegetables are softened.

Stir in the diced tomatoes, tomato paste, dried thyme, dried oregano, salt, and pepper. Cook for another 5-7 minutes, allowing the flavors to meld together. Remove from heat and set aside.

While the ratatouille filling is cooling slightly, prepare the pastry crust. In a large bowl, combine the flour and salt. Cut in the cold cubed butter using a pastry cutter or fork until the mixture resembles coarse crumbs. Gradually add ice water, 1 tablespoon at a time, and mix until the dough comes together.

Roll out the pastry dough on a floured surface to fit the size of your baking dish. Transfer the ratatouille filling into a baking dish. Cover with the rolled-out pastry dough, trimming any excess dough and crimping the edges to seal.

Cut a few slits in the pastry to allow steam to escape during baking.

Place the pot pie in the preheated oven and bake for 35-40 minutes, or until the crust is golden brown and the filling is bubbling.

Let the pot pie cool for a few minutes before serving. Enjoy your delicious ratatouille pot pie!

Feel free to adjust the recipe according to your taste preferences and dietary restrictions. You can also add other vegetables or herbs for extra flavor and variety.

Serve the ratatouille pot pie as a main dish for a satisfying and comforting meal.

Corned Beef and Cabbage Pot Pie

Ingredients:

For the Filling:

- 1 pound (450g) cooked corned beef, diced
- 1 small head cabbage, thinly sliced
- 2 large potatoes, peeled and diced
- 1 onion, diced
- 2 cloves garlic, minced
- 2 tablespoons butter
- 2 tablespoons all-purpose flour
- 1 1/2 cups beef broth
- 1/2 cup milk or cream
- Salt and pepper to taste
- 1 tablespoon chopped fresh parsley (optional)
- 1 tablespoon chopped fresh thyme (optional)

For the Pastry Crust:

- 1 1/2 cups (180g) all-purpose flour
- 1/2 teaspoon salt
- 1/2 cup (113g) unsalted butter, cold and cubed
- 4-6 tablespoons ice water

Instructions:

Preheat your oven to 375°F (190°C).
In a large skillet, melt the butter over medium heat. Add the diced onion and cook until softened, about 5 minutes. Add the minced garlic and cook for an additional minute.
Add the sliced cabbage to the skillet and cook until softened, about 8-10 minutes. Stir in the diced potatoes and cook for another 5 minutes, until slightly tender.
Sprinkle the flour over the vegetables and stir well to coat evenly.
Gradually pour in the beef broth and milk, stirring constantly to prevent lumps from forming. Cook until the mixture thickens, about 5 minutes.
Add the diced corned beef to the skillet and stir to combine. Season with salt and pepper to taste. If desired, add chopped fresh parsley and thyme for extra flavor.

While the filling is cooking, prepare the pastry crust. In a large bowl, combine the flour and salt. Cut in the cold cubed butter using a pastry cutter or fork until the mixture resembles coarse crumbs. Gradually add ice water, 1 tablespoon at a time, and mix until the dough comes together.

Roll out the pastry dough on a floured surface to fit the size of your baking dish. Transfer the corned beef and cabbage filling into a baking dish. Cover with the rolled-out pastry dough, trimming any excess dough and crimping the edges to seal.

Cut a few slits in the pastry to allow steam to escape during baking.

Place the pot pie in the preheated oven and bake for 35-40 minutes, or until the crust is golden brown and the filling is bubbling.

Let the pot pie cool for a few minutes before serving. Enjoy your delicious corned beef and cabbage pot pie!

Feel free to adjust the recipe according to your taste preferences. You can also add other ingredients like carrots or peas for extra flavor and texture. Serve the pot pie as a comforting meal, perfect for St. Patrick's Day or any cozy evening at home.

Chicken and Spinach Pot Pie

Ingredients:

For the Filling:

- 2 cups cooked chicken, shredded or diced
- 4 cups fresh spinach leaves, chopped
- 1 onion, diced
- 2 cloves garlic, minced
- 2 carrots, diced
- 2 stalks celery, diced
- 1 cup frozen peas
- 2 tablespoons butter
- 2 tablespoons all-purpose flour
- 1 1/2 cups chicken broth
- 1/2 cup milk (or non-dairy milk for a creamy vegan option)
- Salt and pepper to taste
- 1 teaspoon dried thyme
- 1 teaspoon dried rosemary

For the Pastry Crust:

- 1 1/2 cups (180g) all-purpose flour
- 1/2 teaspoon salt
- 1/2 cup (113g) unsalted butter or vegan butter, cold and cubed
- 4-6 tablespoons ice water

Instructions:

Preheat your oven to 375°F (190°C).
In a large skillet, melt the butter over medium heat. Add the diced onion, carrots, and celery. Cook until softened, about 5 minutes.
Add the minced garlic to the skillet and cook for an additional minute.
Add the chopped spinach to the skillet and cook until wilted, about 2-3 minutes.
Stir in the cooked chicken and frozen peas. Cook for another 2-3 minutes to heat through.
Sprinkle the flour over the chicken and vegetable mixture. Stir well to coat evenly. Gradually pour in the chicken broth and milk, stirring constantly to prevent lumps from forming. Cook until the mixture thickens, about 5 minutes.

Stir in the dried thyme, dried rosemary, salt, and pepper. Adjust seasoning to taste.

While the filling is cooking, prepare the pastry crust. In a large bowl, combine the flour and salt. Cut in the cold cubed butter using a pastry cutter or fork until the mixture resembles coarse crumbs. Gradually add ice water, 1 tablespoon at a time, and mix until the dough comes together.

Roll out the pastry dough on a floured surface to fit the size of your baking dish. Transfer the chicken and spinach filling into a baking dish. Cover with the rolled-out pastry dough, trimming any excess dough and crimping the edges to seal.

Cut a few slits in the pastry to allow steam to escape during baking.

Place the pot pie in the preheated oven and bake for 35-40 minutes, or until the crust is golden brown and the filling is bubbling.

Let the pot pie cool for a few minutes before serving. Enjoy your delicious chicken and spinach pot pie!

Feel free to adjust the recipe according to your taste preferences and dietary restrictions. You can also add other vegetables or herbs for extra flavor and variety.

Serve the pot pie as a comforting meal for family and friends.

Coconut Curry Vegetable Pot Pie

Ingredients:

For the Filling:

- 1 tablespoon vegetable oil
- 1 onion, diced
- 2 cloves garlic, minced
- 1 tablespoon fresh ginger, grated
- 2 carrots, diced
- 1 bell pepper, diced
- 1 small head cauliflower, cut into small florets
- 1 cup green beans, cut into bite-sized pieces
- 1 can (14 oz) coconut milk
- 2 tablespoons red curry paste
- 1 tablespoon soy sauce (or tamari for gluten-free)
- 1 tablespoon brown sugar (optional, adjust to taste)
- Salt and pepper to taste
- 2 tablespoons cornstarch mixed with 2 tablespoons water (for thickening)

For the Pastry Crust:

- 1 1/2 cups (180g) all-purpose flour
- 1/2 teaspoon salt
- 1/2 cup (113g) unsalted butter or vegan butter, cold and cubed
- 4-6 tablespoons ice water

Instructions:

Preheat your oven to 375°F (190°C).
In a large skillet, heat the vegetable oil over medium heat. Add the diced onion and cook until softened, about 5 minutes. Add the minced garlic and grated ginger, and cook for an additional minute.
Add the diced carrots, bell pepper, cauliflower florets, and green beans to the skillet. Cook, stirring occasionally, until the vegetables are slightly tender, about 5-7 minutes.
In a small bowl, whisk together the coconut milk, red curry paste, soy sauce, and brown sugar (if using). Pour the coconut curry mixture over the vegetables in the skillet. Stir to combine.

Bring the mixture to a simmer and cook for another 5-7 minutes, allowing the flavors to meld together. Season with salt and pepper to taste.

In a small bowl, mix together the cornstarch and water until smooth. Gradually pour the cornstarch mixture into the skillet, stirring constantly, until the sauce thickens slightly. Remove from heat and set aside.

While the filling is cooling slightly, prepare the pastry crust. In a large bowl, combine the flour and salt. Cut in the cold cubed butter using a pastry cutter or fork until the mixture resembles coarse crumbs. Gradually add ice water, 1 tablespoon at a time, and mix until the dough comes together.

Roll out the pastry dough on a floured surface to fit the size of your baking dish. Transfer the coconut curry vegetable filling into a baking dish. Cover with the rolled-out pastry dough, trimming any excess dough and crimping the edges to seal.

Cut a few slits in the pastry to allow steam to escape during baking.

Place the pot pie in the preheated oven and bake for 35-40 minutes, or until the crust is golden brown and the filling is bubbling.

Let the pot pie cool for a few minutes before serving. Enjoy your delicious coconut curry vegetable pot pie!

Feel free to adjust the recipe according to your taste preferences and dietary restrictions. You can also add other vegetables or proteins like tofu or chickpeas for extra flavor and texture. Serve the pot pie as a satisfying and aromatic meal for any occasion.

Apple and Cheddar Pot Pie

Ingredients:

For the Filling:

- 4-5 medium-sized apples, peeled, cored, and thinly sliced (use a mix of sweet and tart varieties)
- 1 tablespoon lemon juice
- 1/4 cup granulated sugar
- 2 tablespoons all-purpose flour
- 1/2 teaspoon ground cinnamon
- Pinch of nutmeg
- Pinch of salt
- 1 cup shredded sharp cheddar cheese
- 2 tablespoons unsalted butter, diced

For the Pastry Crust:

- 1 1/2 cups (180g) all-purpose flour
- 1/2 teaspoon salt
- 1/2 cup (113g) unsalted butter, cold and cubed
- 4-6 tablespoons ice water

Instructions:

Preheat your oven to 375°F (190°C).
In a large bowl, toss the thinly sliced apples with lemon juice to prevent browning.
In a separate bowl, mix together the granulated sugar, flour, ground cinnamon, nutmeg, and salt. Add this mixture to the sliced apples and toss until the apples are evenly coated.
Roll out half of the pastry dough on a floured surface to fit the bottom of your pie dish. Transfer the rolled-out dough to the pie dish and gently press it into the bottom and sides.
Sprinkle half of the shredded cheddar cheese over the bottom of the pastry crust. Arrange the coated apple slices in the pie dish, forming an even layer.
Sprinkle the remaining shredded cheddar cheese over the top of the apple layer. Dot the diced butter evenly over the cheese layer.
Roll out the remaining pastry dough on a floured surface to fit the top of the pie dish. Carefully place it over the apple filling.

Trim any excess dough from the edges and crimp the edges to seal. Cut a few slits in the top crust to allow steam to escape during baking.

Optionally, brush the top crust with a beaten egg for a golden finish.

Place the pot pie in the preheated oven and bake for 40-45 minutes, or until the crust is golden brown and the filling is bubbly.

Allow the pot pie to cool for a few minutes before slicing and serving.

Enjoy your delicious apple and cheddar pot pie warm! You can serve it as is or with a dollop of whipped cream or a scoop of vanilla ice cream for added indulgence.

Feel free to adjust the recipe according to your taste preferences. You can experiment with different types of apples or cheeses to create your preferred flavor profile.

Artichoke and Spinach Pot Pie

Ingredients:

For the Filling:

- 1 tablespoon olive oil
- 1 onion, diced
- 2 cloves garlic, minced
- 1 can (14 oz) artichoke hearts, drained and chopped
- 1 package (10 oz) frozen chopped spinach, thawed and squeezed dry
- 1 cup shredded mozzarella cheese
- 1/2 cup grated Parmesan cheese
- 1 cup ricotta cheese
- 1/4 teaspoon salt
- 1/4 teaspoon black pepper
- 1/4 teaspoon red pepper flakes (optional)
- 1/4 teaspoon dried oregano
- 1/4 teaspoon dried basil
- 1/4 teaspoon dried thyme

For the Pastry Crust:

- 1 1/2 cups (180g) all-purpose flour
- 1/2 teaspoon salt
- 1/2 cup (113g) unsalted butter, cold and cubed
- 4-6 tablespoons ice water

Instructions:

Preheat your oven to 375°F (190°C).
In a large skillet, heat the olive oil over medium heat. Add the diced onion and cook until softened, about 5 minutes. Add the minced garlic and cook for an additional minute.
Add the chopped artichoke hearts to the skillet and cook for 2-3 minutes, stirring occasionally.
Stir in the chopped spinach and cook for another 2-3 minutes, until heated through.
In a large mixing bowl, combine the cooked vegetables with shredded mozzarella cheese, grated Parmesan cheese, ricotta cheese, salt, black pepper, red pepper

flakes (if using), dried oregano, dried basil, and dried thyme. Mix until well combined.

While the filling is cooling slightly, prepare the pastry crust. In a large bowl, combine the flour and salt. Cut in the cold cubed butter using a pastry cutter or fork until the mixture resembles coarse crumbs. Gradually add ice water, 1 tablespoon at a time, and mix until the dough comes together.

Roll out half of the pastry dough on a floured surface to fit the bottom of your pie dish. Transfer the rolled-out dough to the pie dish and gently press it into the bottom and sides.

Spoon the artichoke and spinach filling into the pastry-lined pie dish, spreading it out evenly.

Roll out the remaining pastry dough on a floured surface to fit the top of the pie dish. Carefully place it over the filling.

Trim any excess dough from the edges and crimp the edges to seal. Cut a few slits in the top crust to allow steam to escape during baking.

Place the pot pie in the preheated oven and bake for 35-40 minutes, or until the crust is golden brown and the filling is bubbly.

Let the pot pie cool for a few minutes before slicing and serving.

Enjoy your delicious artichoke and spinach pot pie warm! It's perfect for a cozy dinner or special occasion.

Feel free to adjust the recipe according to your taste preferences. You can add additional herbs or spices to enhance the flavor, or incorporate other vegetables for added variety. Serve the pot pie as a main dish with a side salad or crusty bread for a complete meal.

Chicken and Broccoli Pot Pie

Ingredients:

For the Filling:

- 2 tablespoons unsalted butter
- 1 onion, diced
- 2 cloves garlic, minced
- 2 boneless, skinless chicken breasts, diced
- 2 cups broccoli florets, chopped
- 1 carrot, diced
- 1 celery stalk, diced
- 1/4 cup all-purpose flour
- 2 cups chicken broth
- 1 cup milk (or heavy cream for a richer filling)
- 1 teaspoon dried thyme
- Salt and pepper to taste

For the Pastry Crust:

- 1 1/2 cups (180g) all-purpose flour
- 1/2 teaspoon salt
- 1/2 cup (113g) unsalted butter, cold and cubed
- 4-6 tablespoons ice water

Instructions:

Preheat your oven to 375°F (190°C).

In a large skillet, melt the butter over medium heat. Add the diced onion and cook until softened, about 5 minutes. Add the minced garlic and cook for an additional minute.

Add the diced chicken breasts to the skillet and cook until browned on all sides, about 5-7 minutes.

Stir in the chopped broccoli florets, diced carrot, and diced celery. Cook for another 5 minutes, until the vegetables are slightly tender.

Sprinkle the all-purpose flour over the chicken and vegetable mixture. Stir well to coat evenly.

Gradually pour in the chicken broth and milk, stirring constantly to prevent lumps from forming. Cook until the mixture thickens, about 5 minutes.

Stir in the dried thyme, salt, and pepper. Adjust seasoning to taste.

While the filling is simmering, prepare the pastry crust. In a large bowl, combine the flour and salt. Cut in the cold cubed butter using a pastry cutter or fork until the mixture resembles coarse crumbs. Gradually add ice water, 1 tablespoon at a time, and mix until the dough comes together.

Roll out the pastry dough on a floured surface to fit the size of your baking dish.

Transfer the chicken and broccoli filling into a baking dish. Cover with the rolled-out pastry dough, trimming any excess dough and crimping the edges to seal.

Cut a few slits in the pastry to allow steam to escape during baking.

Place the pot pie in the preheated oven and bake for 35-40 minutes, or until the crust is golden brown and the filling is bubbling.

Let the pot pie cool for a few minutes before serving. Enjoy your delicious chicken and broccoli pot pie!

Feel free to adjust the recipe according to your taste preferences. You can add other vegetables like peas or mushrooms for extra flavor and texture. Serve the pot pie as a satisfying and comforting meal for family and friends.

Chorizo and Potato Pot Pie

Ingredients:

For the Filling:

- 1 tablespoon olive oil
- 1 onion, diced
- 2 cloves garlic, minced
- 8 oz (225g) chorizo sausage, casing removed and crumbled
- 2 large potatoes, peeled and diced
- 1 carrot, diced
- 1 celery stalk, diced
- 2 tablespoons all-purpose flour
- 1 cup chicken or vegetable broth
- 1/2 cup milk
- Salt and pepper to taste
- 1 tablespoon chopped fresh parsley (optional)
- 1 tablespoon chopped fresh thyme (optional)

For the Pastry Crust:

- 1 1/2 cups (180g) all-purpose flour
- 1/2 teaspoon salt
- 1/2 cup (113g) unsalted butter, cold and cubed
- 4-6 tablespoons ice water

Instructions:

Preheat your oven to 375°F (190°C).

In a large skillet, heat the olive oil over medium heat. Add the diced onion and cook until softened, about 5 minutes. Add the minced garlic and cook for an additional minute.

Add the crumbled chorizo sausage to the skillet and cook until browned, breaking it up with a spoon as it cooks.

Stir in the diced potatoes, carrot, and celery. Cook for another 5 minutes, until the vegetables are slightly tender.

Sprinkle the all-purpose flour over the chorizo and vegetable mixture. Stir well to coat evenly.

Gradually pour in the chicken or vegetable broth and milk, stirring constantly to prevent lumps from forming. Cook until the mixture thickens, about 5 minutes. Season with salt and pepper to taste. If desired, add chopped fresh parsley and thyme for extra flavor.

While the filling is simmering, prepare the pastry crust. In a large bowl, combine the flour and salt. Cut in the cold cubed butter using a pastry cutter or fork until the mixture resembles coarse crumbs. Gradually add ice water, 1 tablespoon at a time, and mix until the dough comes together.

Roll out the pastry dough on a floured surface to fit the size of your baking dish. Transfer the chorizo and potato filling into a baking dish. Cover with the rolled-out pastry dough, trimming any excess dough and crimping the edges to seal.

Cut a few slits in the pastry to allow steam to escape during baking.

Place the pot pie in the preheated oven and bake for 35-40 minutes, or until the crust is golden brown and the filling is bubbling.

Let the pot pie cool for a few minutes before serving. Enjoy your delicious chorizo and potato pot pie!

Feel free to adjust the recipe according to your taste preferences. You can add other vegetables or spices to customize the flavor to your liking. Serve the pot pie as a satisfying and comforting meal for any occasion.

Teriyaki Chicken Pot Pie

Ingredients:

For the Filling:

- 2 cups cooked chicken, shredded or diced
- 1 onion, diced
- 2 cloves garlic, minced
- 1 bell pepper, diced
- 1 cup broccoli florets, chopped
- 1 carrot, diced
- 1/2 cup teriyaki sauce
- 1/4 cup soy sauce
- 1 tablespoon sesame oil
- 2 tablespoons cornstarch
- 1/4 cup water
- Salt and pepper to taste
- Sesame seeds and chopped green onions for garnish (optional)

For the Pastry Crust:

- 1 1/2 cups (180g) all-purpose flour
- 1/2 teaspoon salt
- 1/2 cup (113g) unsalted butter or vegetable shortening, cold and cubed
- 4-6 tablespoons ice water

Instructions:

Preheat your oven to 375°F (190°C).

In a large skillet, heat the sesame oil over medium heat. Add the diced onion and cook until softened, about 5 minutes. Add the minced garlic and cook for an additional minute.

Add the diced bell pepper, chopped broccoli, and diced carrot to the skillet. Cook for 5-7 minutes, until the vegetables are slightly tender.

In a small bowl, whisk together the teriyaki sauce, soy sauce, cornstarch, and water until smooth. Pour the mixture into the skillet with the vegetables.

Add the cooked chicken to the skillet. Stir well to combine and simmer for 5-7 minutes, until the sauce thickens.

Season with salt and pepper to taste. Remove from heat and set aside.

While the filling is cooling slightly, prepare the pastry crust. In a large bowl, combine the flour and salt. Cut in the cold cubed butter or vegetable shortening using a pastry cutter or fork until the mixture resembles coarse crumbs.

Gradually add ice water, 1 tablespoon at a time, and mix until the dough comes together.

Roll out the pastry dough on a floured surface to fit the size of your baking dish.

Transfer the teriyaki chicken filling into a baking dish. Cover with the rolled-out pastry dough, trimming any excess dough and crimping the edges to seal.

Cut a few slits in the pastry to allow steam to escape during baking.

Optionally, brush the top crust with a beaten egg for a golden finish.

Place the pot pie in the preheated oven and bake for 35-40 minutes, or until the crust is golden brown and the filling is bubbling.

Let the pot pie cool for a few minutes before serving. Garnish with sesame seeds and chopped green onions, if desired.

Enjoy your delicious teriyaki chicken pot pie! Serve it as a comforting and satisfying meal for any occasion.

Greek Lamb Pot Pie

Ingredients:

For the Filling:

- 1 tablespoon olive oil
- 1 onion, diced
- 2 cloves garlic, minced
- 1 pound (450g) ground lamb
- 1 teaspoon dried oregano
- 1 teaspoon dried thyme
- 1 teaspoon ground cumin
- 1/2 teaspoon ground cinnamon
- 1/4 teaspoon ground nutmeg
- Salt and pepper to taste
- 1 cup diced tomatoes (fresh or canned)
- 1 cup cooked chickpeas (canned or cooked from dry)
- 1/2 cup chopped kalamata olives
- 1/4 cup chopped fresh parsley
- 1/4 cup chopped fresh mint
- 1/2 cup crumbled feta cheese

For the Pastry Crust:

- 1 1/2 cups (180g) all-purpose flour
- 1/2 teaspoon salt
- 1/2 cup (113g) unsalted butter, cold and cubed
- 4-6 tablespoons ice water

Instructions:

Preheat your oven to 375°F (190°C).
In a large skillet, heat the olive oil over medium heat. Add the diced onion and cook until softened, about 5 minutes. Add the minced garlic and cook for an additional minute.
Add the ground lamb to the skillet. Cook, breaking it up with a spoon, until browned and cooked through, about 8-10 minutes.
Stir in the dried oregano, dried thyme, ground cumin, ground cinnamon, ground nutmeg, salt, and pepper. Cook for another minute to toast the spices.

Add the diced tomatoes, cooked chickpeas, and chopped kalamata olives to the skillet. Stir well to combine and simmer for 5-7 minutes, allowing the flavors to meld together.

Remove the skillet from the heat and stir in the chopped fresh parsley and mint. Adjust seasoning to taste.

While the filling is cooling slightly, prepare the pastry crust. In a large bowl, combine the flour and salt. Cut in the cold cubed butter using a pastry cutter or fork until the mixture resembles coarse crumbs. Gradually add ice water, 1 tablespoon at a time, and mix until the dough comes together.

Roll out half of the pastry dough on a floured surface to fit the bottom of your pie dish. Transfer the rolled-out dough to the pie dish and gently press it into the bottom and sides.

Spoon the lamb filling into the pastry-lined pie dish, spreading it out evenly. Crumble the feta cheese over the top of the lamb filling.

Roll out the remaining pastry dough on a floured surface to fit the top of the pie dish. Carefully place it over the filling.

Trim any excess dough from the edges and crimp the edges to seal. Cut a few slits in the top crust to allow steam to escape during baking.

Place the pot pie in the preheated oven and bake for 35-40 minutes, or until the crust is golden brown and the filling is bubbling.

Let the pot pie cool for a few minutes before serving. Enjoy your delicious Greek lamb pot pie!

Feel free to adjust the recipe according to your taste preferences. You can add other Mediterranean ingredients like sun-dried tomatoes, artichoke hearts, or roasted red peppers for extra flavor. Serve the pot pie as a main dish for a satisfying and flavorful meal.

Macaroni and Cheese Pot Pie

Ingredients:

For the Macaroni and Cheese Filling:

- 8 oz (about 2 cups) elbow macaroni
- 2 tablespoons unsalted butter
- 2 tablespoons all-purpose flour
- 2 cups whole milk
- 2 cups shredded sharp cheddar cheese
- 1/2 cup grated Parmesan cheese
- Salt and pepper to taste
- 1/4 teaspoon garlic powder (optional)
- 1/4 teaspoon mustard powder (optional)

For the Pastry Crust:

- 1 1/2 cups (180g) all-purpose flour
- 1/2 teaspoon salt
- 1/2 cup (113g) unsalted butter, cold and cubed
- 4-6 tablespoons ice water

Instructions:

Preheat your oven to 375°F (190°C).
Cook the elbow macaroni according to the package instructions until al dente. Drain and set aside.
In a large saucepan, melt the butter over medium heat. Stir in the flour and cook for 1-2 minutes to make a roux.
Gradually whisk in the milk, stirring constantly to prevent lumps from forming. Cook until the mixture thickens, about 5-7 minutes.
Reduce the heat to low and stir in the shredded cheddar cheese and grated Parmesan cheese until melted and smooth. Season with salt, pepper, garlic powder, and mustard powder, if using.
Add the cooked elbow macaroni to the cheese sauce, stirring until evenly coated.
While the macaroni and cheese filling is cooling slightly, prepare the pastry crust. In a large bowl, combine the flour and salt. Cut in the cold cubed butter using a pastry cutter or fork until the mixture resembles coarse crumbs. Gradually add ice water, 1 tablespoon at a time, and mix until the dough comes together.

Roll out half of the pastry dough on a floured surface to fit the bottom of your pie dish. Transfer the rolled-out dough to the pie dish and gently press it into the bottom and sides.

Spoon the macaroni and cheese filling into the pastry-lined pie dish, spreading it out evenly.

Roll out the remaining pastry dough on a floured surface to fit the top of the pie dish. Carefully place it over the macaroni and cheese filling.

Trim any excess dough from the edges and crimp the edges to seal. Cut a few slits in the top crust to allow steam to escape during baking.

Optionally, brush the top crust with a beaten egg for a golden finish.

Place the pot pie in the preheated oven and bake for 35-40 minutes, or until the crust is golden brown and the filling is bubbling.

Let the pot pie cool for a few minutes before serving. Enjoy your delicious macaroni and cheese pot pie!

Feel free to adjust the recipe according to your taste preferences. You can add breadcrumbs or extra cheese on top of the filling for added texture and flavor. Serve the pot pie as a comforting and indulgent meal for family and friends.

Thai Red Curry Chicken Pot Pie

Ingredients:

For the Filling:

- 2 tablespoons vegetable oil
- 1 onion, diced
- 2 cloves garlic, minced
- 1 red bell pepper, diced
- 1 yellow bell pepper, diced
- 1 carrot, diced
- 1 cup broccoli florets, chopped
- 1 lb (450g) boneless, skinless chicken breast, diced
- 3 tablespoons Thai red curry paste
- 1 can (13.5 oz) coconut milk
- 1 tablespoon fish sauce (or soy sauce for a vegetarian option)
- 1 tablespoon brown sugar (optional)
- Salt and pepper to taste
- Fresh cilantro leaves for garnish (optional)

For the Pastry Crust:

- 1 1/2 cups (180g) all-purpose flour
- 1/2 teaspoon salt
- 1/2 cup (113g) unsalted butter, cold and cubed
- 4-6 tablespoons ice water

Instructions:

Preheat your oven to 375°F (190°C).
In a large skillet, heat the vegetable oil over medium heat. Add the diced onion and cook until softened, about 5 minutes. Add the minced garlic and cook for an additional minute.
Add the diced red and yellow bell peppers, diced carrot, and chopped broccoli to the skillet. Cook for 5-7 minutes, until the vegetables are slightly tender.
Push the vegetables to one side of the skillet and add the diced chicken breast to the other side. Cook until the chicken is browned on all sides, about 5-7 minutes.
Stir in the Thai red curry paste and cook for another minute, until fragrant.
Pour in the coconut milk, fish sauce (or soy sauce), and brown sugar (if using). Stir well to combine all ingredients.

Simmer the mixture for 10-15 minutes, stirring occasionally, until the sauce thickens slightly and the chicken is cooked through. Season with salt and pepper to taste.

While the filling is simmering, prepare the pastry crust. In a large bowl, combine the flour and salt. Cut in the cold cubed butter using a pastry cutter or fork until the mixture resembles coarse crumbs. Gradually add ice water, 1 tablespoon at a time, and mix until the dough comes together.

Roll out the pastry dough on a floured surface to fit the size of your baking dish. Transfer the Thai red curry chicken filling into a baking dish. Cover with the rolled-out pastry dough, trimming any excess dough and crimping the edges to seal.

Cut a few slits in the pastry to allow steam to escape during baking.

Place the pot pie in the preheated oven and bake for 35-40 minutes, or until the crust is golden brown and the filling is bubbling.

Let the pot pie cool for a few minutes before serving. Garnish with fresh cilantro leaves, if desired.

Enjoy your delicious Thai red curry chicken pot pie! Serve it as a flavorful and unique meal for any occasion.

www.ingramcontent.com/pod-product-compliance
Lightning Source LLC
LaVergne TN
LVHW081601060526
838201LV00054B/2005